The Map of My Life

The Map of My Life

The Story of Emma Humphreys

Edited by Julie Bindel
& Harriet Wistrich

Astraia Press

First published 2003 by Astraia Press
55 Rathcoole Gardens, London N8 9NE
© EHMP 2003

British Library Cataloguing in Publication Data
A catalogue record for this book is available
from the British Library

ISBN 0 954 6341 0 1

Printed and bound in Great Britain by
CLE Print Ltd, Huntingdon, Cambridgeshire

Acknowledgements

We would like to express our gratitude and thanks to the following:

All of the contributors to this book, including Beatrix Campbell and Judith Jones, Julie McNamara, Rosie Fitzharris and Vera Baird.

All of those who have helped in the production of this book – Cheryl Stafford, Chris Fayers, Carolanne Lyme, Karen Shook, Sheila Burton, Barbara Nicholls, Lillian Mohin, Julie Newman, Rosie Fitzharris, Jo Thompson, Ian Lazarus – and Lucy Edkins for the painting used on the cover. We are particularly indebted to Ju Gosling, who has creatively managed the production of this book, and without whose patience, attention to detail and calm perseverance, we would never have met the ridiculously tight publishing deadline we set ourselves only six months ago.

John and Rebecca Humphreys, Joan Scanlon, all of the members of the EHMP, in particular Claire Lazarus, Ellen Reynolds and Linda Regan, Patricia Holmes, Chris Root, Bridget Irving and Sarah Maguire, Sandra McNeill.

The Maypole Fund and the Emma Humphreys Memorial Prize for providing funds towards the production of this book.

We are sure that Emma would wish to give a very special 'thank you' to all of the members of the Justice for Women campaign, to Southall Black Sisters, and to each and every one of you who supported her bid for freedom.

Last but not least, Peggy and Tiger for their cuddles, reassurances and loyalty.

Contents

Foreword

It is right that Emma Humphreys' life should be celebrated. First, her sensitive and sharp writing is remarkable as the work of a young woman whose life was almost wholly one of abandonment and abuse. How did she keep that self-sufficient individual voice alive despite the rapes, the cruelty and the beatings, and the interminable incarceration imposed on her when she, for self-preservation, once, and only once, struck back? How did Emma speak so clearly, even from the drug and alcohol haven into which these mistreatments shipwrecked her, and which eventually claimed her life?

Many days, when I wait for the W7 bus from Crouch End town hall, on my way either to the Courts or to the House of Commons, I sit on the bench put there in Emma's memory by Justice for Women. "Campaigner and Writer" – as the plaque asserts – she certainly was, from quite a different dimension to many of us. We may, at some stage, have suffered poor treatment in our own lives, but most of us have eased our problems and occupy the balanced world of the chattering classes long before we start to work for others. Here was a woman, still gripped by chaotic self-image, hopelessness and depression, who nonetheless emerged into our campaigning world and enriched it, even as her problems tormented her.

It is ironic that, whatever circulation this volume achieves, it will not exceed that of the other book in which Emma is a star. For her case is a key legal precedent in the defence of provocation. Her name and life story are at a much-thumbed page in every copy of the Law Reports, the All England Reports and the Criminal Appeal Reports, most of them owned by lawyers whose histories are remote from the hard-knock world that she inhabited.

I wonder what, when having a Bacardi Breezer on a sunny day in paradise, she thinks of this? Is Emma amused when grave, grey, bewigged Etonian men grapple, in London's Court of Appeal, with the juristic implications of being put into an abnormal state of mind by appalling treatment from men – as explained in the case of *R v Emma Humphreys 1995 4 All ER.1*?

Some trials today would make Emma angry. In almost every murder trial, where the defendant is a woman, the judge will assert that it is 'not a battered woman case'. It is 'not a battered woman case' because she could have left – even though it was her's and her children's home. 'Not a battered woman case' because she hit him back, once in a hundred times, thereby moving into the 'stormy marriage/six of one – half a dozen of the other' category. It is 'not a battered woman case' because she once cursed a policeman she'd called out and got arrested herself, forfeiting judicial sympathy to officers who have a hard task dealing with 'domestics'.

It is 'not a battered woman case' if she hasn't straightaway set out, verbatim, every act of abuse that he inflicted on her to the police – and any additional allegations, perhaps elicited from her after weeks of engagement by a supportive solicitor, will make her a liar, trying to bandwagon on compassion. Sometimes, it is 'not a battered woman case' precisely because she has killed him; since that makes him unavailable to give his version, which it is presumed would be that he didn't batter her.

What is different between these trials and Emma's trial is the law. First, there was the understanding by Lord Taylor, in *Ahluwalia*, that self-control was not always lost immediately after provocation but could fail later, when the impact trickled through. That has since shielded from murder convictions many women who killed when their partner was asleep, nurturing his energy for the next beating.

In turn, the *Ahluwalia* judgment opened the way to arguing before different judges in Emma's case that provocation, since it did not always have immediate effect, could be cumulative. Her first ground of appeal was that the trial judge had told the jury that the only things they could treat as capable of having provoked her to kill were those that Armitage did immediately before the killing. The last of those was to threaten to rape her. That was bad enough, but was much more provocative in the context of a conversation some hours before, in which Armitage had talked to friends about a "gang bang" with her. Justice had not been done at trial, by preventing the jury from seeing it in that way.

The other successful ground of appeal was that, since the law requires the defendant's loss of self-control to be checked against the presumed response of "a reasonable man" subject to the same provocation, relevant characteristics of the defendant ought to be allocated to the reasonable man as well. It was well-established that youth and sex were relevant to a fair application of that check. You cannot judge a 17-year-old girl by the standard of self-control of a "reasonable man"of 40. But Emma's case established that vulnerabilities, whether innate, or, as in her case, caused by her treatment by Armitage and his predecessor men in her life, should also be attributed to the reasonable person, so as to judge the defendant fairly.

We regarded ourselves as 'lucky' that Emma was so young, and had been so ill-treated, that establishing these principles looked like stand-alone compassion. The dangerous backlash that might have followed if we had had to refer to the gendered nature of domestic violence never came into play. Now Emma's case often overcomes that backlash when it is exhibited by male trial judges asserting that this is 'not a battered women case'. Evidence emerges of degradation, humiliation, sexual abuse and violence, and must be called cumulative provocation. A woman's conduct in killing must be checked against a "reasonable person" who is as vulnerable as this treatment has made her. The Court of Appeal says so!

Emma's case also significantly contributed to mainstream politics. During and after her case, a number of MPs from all parties began to take particular notice of what feminists had been saying for years: that domestic violence is not taken seriously in cases of battered women who kill; or when men kill their partners after years of abusing them. Emma engendered empathy amongst those who needed a moving, personal story to understand the devastation caused by violence, abuse and prison. This was a significant factor in leading to the issue of the defence of provocation being put before the Law Commission in 2003.

I would like to think of Lord Taylor, a great judge who died too soon, my terrific friend, the late, great Helen Grindrod QC, who led me in the case and Emma, having a few more Bacardi Breezers in paradise, toasting the precedents they made successively, but together.

Vera Baird, QC MP

The Map of My Life

I'm angry
Yes I'm very fucking angry
But it's not up close
Up close up is sadness and tears welling up
But I've cried so much today
My head hurts

You
You who drugged me up
And did god only knows what to me
A stray fourteen year old
Did you think it was fun feeding me pills?
Let me collapse in the shower
Next thing I know
You're trying to hold me up and dress me on the bed
What did you tell me
Through the haze of drugs?
Koolade, that was it
We needed to go to the shop for koolade.
How kind of you to dress me
And help me stagger out of your apartment
Me, fourteen, drugged, wasn't thinking
Let you prop me up in the freezing snow
Must have been at least minus fifteen degrees
And I fucking stood there for a while
All of about a couple of minutes
I couldn't stand, didn't have the co-ordination
So I slumped in the snow
Like a good believing child
As I waited for you to return
From a house you said you were going to for money
You bastard
You may have left me for dead
But here I am today
Had your fun did you?
And then did you get scared?
Scared that you'd nearly killed me with pills?

Fucking, cowardly bastard
I was bleeding down below
But I don't want to fucking know what you did
I know enough about you to know I hate you
OK. You're just one
But I remember you clearly
I never thought I could get to help
But I did
It's a wonder I wasn't killed
Wobbling my way across
One of the biggest roads in Edmonton
I made it all right
And got help with getting a taxi
I came back to haunt you
You fucking prick
Outside your apartment door
I sliced five inches up my arm
I call my scars the map of my life
Yours is still very much there
A bleeding nose from falling
Blood rushing out of my arm
Blood between my legs
Dumb-struck weren't you?
Prick
Tried to stop the flow of blood
And threw me in another taxi
That was the end for you and I
I hope it was the end of you
Playing with fourteen year old girls

It didn't end there for me
And you weren't even the first
Mother fucking bastard to mess with me
You certainly weren't the last.

Trevor was the last
And rest his soul
That people like you
Contributed to his death.

Introduction

On the morning of 8 July 1995, the *Guardian* newspaper came through our letterbox. The whole of the front page was taken up with one story, headlined: "Quashed murder verdict gives hope to abused women." Below, a half-page portrait photograph of a smiling, somewhat bewildered looking young woman with the caption: "Freed on Appeal, Emma Humphreys outside the Appeal Court in London yesterday. She said, 'In my heart, it wasn't murder.'" In our spare room that same morning Emma Humphreys was waking up, having spent her first night in over ten years sleeping in a room without a lock on the door.

It was about three years earlier that an envelope had dropped through the same letterbox, addressed to Julie Bindel of Justice for Women. On prison-headed notepaper came a brilliantly articulated plea from a 24-year-old woman who had already spent the last seven years in prison. She asked, in terms that could have touched the most hard-hearted, if we would help her to fight her murder conviction? The long battle that we embarked upon led us eventually to the front-page news stories. It was an historic victory, signifying the power of feminist campaigning.

Almost exactly three very hard and painful years following that victory, on 11 July 1998, we went to Emma's flat, about a mile away from our home. Unusually, we had not been able to get hold of Emma over the phone for over 24 hours. On receiving no response to our knocks at the door, we used the spare keys that she had entrusted us with to enter the flat. Her kitten Tiger danced playfully about the flat, her food bowl still full. On her bed, curled comfortably in a peaceful position, lay Emma Humphreys, but she was not asleep. She had died, accidentally, of an overdose of the medication that she had become addicted to whilst in prison.

We have put together this collection of Emma's writing and other contributions about her life for a number of reasons. First and foremost, Emma believed that others could learn from her life story, and we share that belief. This book will appeal to a wide constituency of readers – survivors, students of feminism, law, sociology and criminology, professionals working with abused adults and children, feminist activists and advocates, lawyers, social workers, psychiatrists, health practitioners, foster parents, those working within the criminal justice system and others.

During Emma's three years of freedom she expressed many times the desire to write a book about her life, and we tried to help her. But the chaotic prescription drug- and alcohol-befuddled life that followed so many years of abuse and institutionalisation inhibited the discipline required to sit down and map out her life in writing.

What we didn't know until after her death was that, in fact, Emma had already written her story. Just after she died Emma's father, John, told us that Emma had asked him to store some volumes of papers in his loft. Amongst these was a series of diaries that she had kept as a teenager before her imprisonment, and a 30-page closely typed account written by Emma from Durham prison in 1988 telling her life story. In particular, it provided a detailed account of the events that led up to her meeting Trevor Armitage. It went on to describe the build-up of pressures that culminated in that fateful night in February 1985 when, following his threat of rape, she killed him.

What we don't know is whether Emma had simply forgotten about the existence of this story, which she must have written intensively over a short period, fairly near the start of her sentence at the high-security prison in Durham. Or did she recall its existence, but now had a different story to tell? Having worked very closely with Emma in the preparation for her appeal and through our feminist campaigning and media work, it is noticeable that her perspective on her life in the story written in 1988 is different from the one that we came to know when working with her between 1992 and 1995.

The purpose of the earlier account seemed to be an explanation of how she had come to kill a man, written in a prison context where there may have been a great deal of pressure on her to 'engage with her offending behaviour'. By 1992, however, when Emma first wrote to us at the Justice for Women campaign, there had been widespread media coverage of the feminist campaigns around Sara Thornton, Kiranjt Ahluwalia and other battered women who had killed. The result of that campaigning was that there was a greater sympathy and understanding of the circumstances that can drive a woman to kill her abuser, as well as an awareness of the discrimination that exists in the criminal justice system.

In fact, Emma wrote important accounts of her life in a number of different ways and styles, and from a range of different perspectives. We have therefore edited together what we believe are some of the most interesting and powerfully expressive extracts from her writing.

We open with 'The Diaries', a chapter containing extracts from Emma's diaries. These appear to have been started as therapeutic device when she was a teenager incarcerated in a youth detention centre in Canada, after having run away from a violent home, from foster care and from children's homes into an exploitative world of drugs and child sexual abuse. Many of these entries reveal the level of despair and desperation experienced by Emma during these crucial years. The diary entries continue right up to her meeting with Armitage, and the abuse that she experienced within their relationship. We have juxtaposed some of these diary entries with contemporaneous extracts from reports written by those charged with her care, revealing a sometimes judgemental and inappropriate response to an abused child.

In the chapter entitled 'Telling My Story', we have reproduced (in edited form) the account that Emma wrote from Durham prison of her young life and of her relationship with Trevor Armitage. We consider that this is one of the most original, direct and powerful first-hand accounts to describe the life of a young woman abused in street prostitution, as well as a crucial documentation of the build-up to the homicide.

The chapter entitled 'Letters from Prison' reproduces extracts from some of the correspondence that we received from Emma during the three years of working with her in the build-up to her campaign and appeal. They also show the obstacles faced by Emma from the authorities as a result of her challenging her conviction and life sentence.

In addition to the various extracts from Emma's own writing, we have included contributions from others which we feel add important components to Emma's story. In the chapter 'Justice for Women', we invited the journalist Beatrix Campbell and child abuse expert Judith Jones to provide an overview of the political context in which Emma's campaign for justice emerged. Emma's story is also about the power of feminist campaigning. Despite all of the tragedy of Emma's life, there is also so much to celebrate. We want her life and her battle for justice to be an inspiration to others.

'Not a Suicide Note' reproduces a speech by Harriet Wistrich at the first memorial event, held a few months after Emma died. It describes the pain and struggle to survive in an unfamiliar world following Emma's release from prison, after a lifetime of abuse and institutionalisation. This contribution also questions the 'inevitability' of Emma's death.

Julie McNamara, a performer and mental health activist who befriended Emma following her release from prison, has provided an introduction to her song, 'Fly Like an Eagle', written in dedication to Emma's life.

Finally, 'For Emma', the chapter from Rosie Fitzharris, who became Emma's best friend during her last three years, provides a deeply intimate account of Emma's day-to-day life. It offers an insight into who Emma was, away from the gaze of the media, professionals, and even feminist campaigners!

In order to assist the reader in placing the various contributions in times, places and contexts, we provide below a short biography of the life of Emma. You will also find a short explanation of the various individuals referred to throughout this book.

Emma was at Holloway prison for the last period of her imprisonment, during the two-and-a-half years when she was working with the Justice for Women campaign towards her appeal. The education department employed people from outside the prison to run classes of various types, and amongst these was a writers' group run by Tom Sheerin.

At her memorial, Tom described Emma's contribution to the group:

"She was very special. She used to come breezing in and out, and no matter what was happening, somehow everyone made space for her. Although she seemed like a wild young thing on some levels, on other levels she came across as very wise, as an old soul, as though she knew a lot more than the rest of us. That's how I will always remember her, as well as her great sense of humour in the midst of some terrible things that were happening to her.

"She wouldn't read her own stuff for a long time. She would give it to someone else to read, which was quite sad because when she did start reading, she had a beautiful voice and she read with considerable dignity and pace. She always made a great impression."

Emma clearly found poetry a creative device to distil her thoughts and feelings about a range of experiences in her life. Indeed, the title of this book comes from her poem, 'I call my scars the map of my life'. You will find her poems placed throughout this book. They clearly reflect the main themes that were occupying Emma during this period; sanity and madness; freedom and imprisonment; memories and experience:

The Borderline

To slip over the edge
Would be like
To carelessly write
Over the edges of this paper.

If you want to know
Where my sanity lies,
Just feel the edges
Of this paper you are holding.

That's where it lies,
My dividing line —
The absolute borderline
Between my sanity and insanity.

Within these four corners
And sharp pointed edges
I shall contain my composure
Using available ink.

This safe place I've found
Is as precious as my soul;
I can write down my mind
In simple As, Bs and Cs.

I can be totally me
And totally selfish.
I can place dried-up tears
And recreate wiped-out smiles.

And now that I've found
Just where my borderline lies.
I shall search for nothing more
Than the freedom to feel and write.

Emma Humphreys
A Short Biography

Emma Humphreys was born on 30 October 1967 in Dolgellau, Wales.

Her mother was Pamela June Ackroyd, who had left her home town in Nottingham at around the age of 18 to work in hotels in the North Wales holiday resort. She met John Humphreys, a local working class lad, and became pregnant by him. They had three children together, Rebecca, followed by Emma, and then Abigail.

At the age of five, Emma's parents separated and June returned to Nottingham, taking the three children with her. John decided to follow later on his own. June had a number of relationships with men, worked at a bar, and, when Emma was aged ten, she met Al Somerville, a Canadian who worked on the North Sea oil rigs. They married, and emigrated with the three girls to Alberta in Canada.

Al was extremely violent and abusive towards June and her children, and, isolated from her friends and family in the UK, Emma's mother retreated into an alcoholic chaos. She appears to have turned against her middle daughter, Emma, who had once been her closest child.

From around the age of 12, Emma started running away from home. She would hitchhike lifts from men who would sexually abuse her, and in that way she got drawn into the world of prostitution and pornography, becoming increasingly suicidal. From the ages of 12 to 15, Emma was in and out of children's homes, foster care and youth detention, attending school irregularly. It was during this period that she started keeping a diary.

At around the age of 15, Emma's father John made contact with Emma. He had apparently attempted to remain in contact when the family left for Canada, but Emma's mother had hidden the cards and presents that he'd sent. Arrangements were made for Emma to return to England to live with her father.

However, by this time John was remarried, to Elizabeth, and had started a new family. When Emma returned to England she was already a very damaged and unruly teenager, and the relationship between her and her father's new family quickly broke down. She then moved into live with her maternal grandmother, Bertha Elizabeth Ackroyd, who also lived in Notting-ham with her sister, Pamela Ackroyd. Not surprisingly, Emma did not fit in well with her grandmother and great aunt, and begged to be allowed to return to Canada to be with her family there.

Her father and grandmother bought her an air ticket, and in the spring of 1984 Emma returned to Canada. The immigration authorities would not allow her to re-enter the country. She was allowed to stay overnight with one of her foster mothers, before being due to be deported again to England. However, Emma went on the run for several weeks before being placed on a plane and flown back to England. She then had no choice but to return to Nottingham to stay with her grandmother. She lived there for a few weeks, but soon became bored, and one day decided to pack her bags and leave home.

It was then that Emma became embroiled in street prostitution in Nottingham. She soon met Trevor Armitage, a punter twice her age, who invited her to live with him. Although in a relationship with Trevor, Emma continued to work daily as a street prostitute, and Trevor took her money and controlled her movements. The relationship also became very violent, and Emma started drinking heavily at this time. Emma was arrested on a number of occasions for soliciting, and also on one occasion for causing criminal damage to Trevor's home. She was initially bailed and required to stay in a bail hostel, but breached the rules and therefore, at the beginning of February 1985, was remanded in custody to Risley Prison.

On 21 February 1985 Emma appeared in court and received a two-year conditional discharge; she was released into 'the care' of Trevor Armitage. On 23 February, Emma's mother telephoned the police from Canada to say that she had received a call from her daughter to the effect that she was afraid of Trevor Armitage and could the police attend? Police officers did attempt to go to the house, but could not gain access. On the night of 25 February 1985, Emma stabbed Trevor Armitage and then summoned help. She was arrested, and Trevor was pronounced dead.

Emma's trial, which lasted four days, took place at Nottingham Crown Court in December 1985. She was unable to give evidence in her defence, and therefore relied on an interview given to the police that contained a number of inaccuracies. A psychiatrist, Dr Tarsh, who was the only witness appearing for the defence, gave evidence supporting the partial defence of manslaughter on the grounds of provocation. The jury took only two hours to return a unanimous verdict of guilty of murder, and Emma was sentenced to be detained 'at Her Majesty's pleasure', a mandatory life sentence.

In January 1986, Emma's solicitor lodged a ground of appeal which was rejected by the single judge at the Court of Appeal. In April 1986, Emma signed an abandonment of all proceedings in the Court of Appeal.

Emma commenced her life sentence in HMP Durham high-security prison, where reports indicate that she was initially "very depressed and extremely withdrawn". However, by 1988, reports written suggest that "she had matured and had become more confident and self assured". Interestingly, it was around this time that Emma wrote her account of the lead-up to the homicide which appears later in this book.

In February 1989 Emma was transferred to HMP Styal (a medium-secure prison), where reports of her progress were good. However, she soon made allegations of sexual harassment against a male member of staff, and was therefore transferred to New Hall prison. In September 1989 the parole board recommended her for transfer to open conditions, although government ministers instead decided that she required a further 12 months in New Hall. In January 1992 the parole board met again and recommended her transfer to open prison, and in April 1992 she was transferred to HMP Drake Hall.

In September 1992, Emma made contact with the Justice for Women campaign, who took up her case.

In November 1992, allegations were made by another inmate that Emma had threatened her with a knife, and she was transferred to HMP Holloway. An investigation into the allegations 'proved inconclusive', and Emma remained at Holloway for three months before being transferred to another open prison, HMP East Sutton Park.

In May 1993, on Emma's first home leave visit from East Sutton Park to Nottingham, she failed to return on time and was later discovered unconscious, having collapsed from taking an overdose of antidepressants. She later disclosed that she had been picked up by a man at Kings Cross and raped. As a result she was then returned to Holloway Prison, where she remained until her appeal in 1995.

In January 1995, Emma's application for leave to appeal and to nullify her previous abandonment of the appeal proceedings was heard at the Court of Appeal and granted.

In June 1995, supported by a large demonstration organised by the Justice for Women campaign, Emma's case was heard at the Court of Appeal. Following two days of legal argument, judgment was reserved for a week. On 7 July 1995 Emma's conviction of murder was quashed, and a conviction of manslaughter by reason of provocation was substituted. Emma walked free from the Court of Appeal to the cheers of supporters and front-page news headlines.

Following her release from prison, Emma initially stayed at the home of Julie and Harriet, awaiting a placement that had been arranged at a residential therapeutic home for damaged young adults, run by the Richmond Fellowship in Sevenoaks, Kent. She remained there for a few weeks, but was eventually asked to leave following numerous incidents of "disruptive behaviour". Emma stayed in bed and breakfast, before being found a placement at a hostel for people with mental health problems in Crouch End. After a few weeks there she was also asked to leave, having broken most of the hostel centre's rules.

For the next few months Emma stayed in a variety of bed and breakfast homes and hostels. She was drinking heavily, using illegal drugs and going down hill fast. Around this time she was raped by a man who forced his way into the room she was staying in at a homeless hostel, and she reported the incident to the police. She was eventually found accommodation in another homeless hostel in Hackney, where she remained for a few months before being offered her own flat near Crouch End in London.

Emma lived the last 15 months of her life in this flat, part of the time with a 'boyfriend', Rico, whom she'd met at the last homeless hostel. On 30 October 1997 she celebrated her 30th birthday, and was given a kitten, Tiger, who came to live with her. She asked Rico to move out, and eventually made allegations of rape against him which were due to be investigated by the police. In June 1998 she came away to Italy on her first holiday following release from prison with Julie, Harriet, Rosie and Cheryl.

Emma died on 11 July 1998. A subsequent inquest determined that she died as a result of an accidental overdose of the medication prescribed by her doctor.

List of people mentioned

Adam Sommerville	Al and June's son and Emma's half-brother
Amelia Rossiter	Convicted of murdering her violent husband, freed on appeal in 1991
Al Sommerville	Emma's stepfather
Abigail Humphreys	Emma's younger sister
Cheryl Stafford	Friend of Emma and member of Justice for Women
Elizabeth	John Humphreys' second wife
Hannana Siddiqui	Member of Southall Black Sisters
Harriet Wistrich	Friend of Emma and member of Justice for Women
Helen Grindrod	Leading counsel (QC) at Emma's appeal
Jane Taubman	Member of Justice for Women
Janet Gardner	Convicted of the manslaughter of her violent partner and freed after one year on appeal
John Humphreys	Emma's father
Julie Bindel	Friend of Emma and member of Justice for Women
Julie Syramis	Emma's girlfriend in prison
Julie McNamara	Friend of Emma
June	Emma's mother
Kiranjit Ahluwalia	Convicted of murdering her violent husband and freed after retrial in 1992

Linda Regan	Counselled Emma in prison in the build-up to appeal
Liz Kelly	Member of Justice for Women
Matthew Humphreys	Emma's half-brother (John Humphrey's son)
Mitch Egan	HM Prison Lifer Unit
Moonie	Emma's pet cockatiel in prison
Nana (Bertha Ackroyd)	Emma's maternal grandmother
Nickie	Emma's friend in prison
Paul Newell	HM Prison Lifer Unit
Peggy	Julie, Harriet and Rosie's dog
Rebecca Humphreys	Emma's older sister
Rico	Emma's 'boyfriend', whom she met in a hostel and later accused of rape
Rohit Sanghvi	Emma, Kiranjit and Janet Gardner's solicitor
Rosie Fitzharris	Emma's closest friend following her release from prison
Sandra McNeill	Member of Justice for Women
Sara Thornton	Convicted of murdering her violent husband and freed after retrial in 1996
Simon Sommerville	Al and June's son and Emma's half-brother
Susan	Emma's best friend in Canada
Tom Sheerin	Emma's creative writing teacher in Holloway
Toni/Anthony	Pimp who 'befriended' Emma in Nottingham
Trevor Armitage	Pimp and violent 'boyfriend' of Emma whom she killed in 1985
Vera Baird	Barrister at Emma's appeal

Part I

From Childhood to Prison

(Left to right) Emma's sisters Rebecca and Abigail with Emma in Nottingham, early 1970s.

1: The Diaries

Amongst the papers that Emma asked her dad to store in his home were three ring binders of diary entries. The first entry appears to have been made in December 1982, when Emma had just turned 15 and was living at Westfield, a diagnostic and treatment residential children's home in Edmonton, Canada. The last entry is made in Nottingham, England in January 1985, just a few weeks before she killed Trevor Armitage.

It would appear from some of the early diary entries made when Emma was in residential care that she may have been encouraged to keep a diary, which could also be read by the residential workers to monitor her feelings. In fact, some of the entries actually contain comments written by the care workers. However, whatever the initial intention of the diaries, they clearly became a therapeutic device for Emma, and occasionally also a means to explore more creatively her inner world. It becomes clear that the diary was her friend, perhaps the only person that could understand her, and at times that relationship is intense.

Official documents that were sent to Emma's solicitor in England from the Canadian social services indicate that Emma was placed in a range of childcare institutions from the age of 13 . We know that her home life had become very chaotic. Her stepfather, Al Sommerville, was sadistically violent. Both he and her mother had become serious alcoholics. Emma started running away from home from around the age of 12, and, like many young runaways, she quickly got drawn in to the exploitative world of drink, drugs and child prostitution.

We have included, chronologically, extracts from the psychological assessments of Emma made at the time, alongside some of the diary entries. They provide some clues as to the outside pressures on Emma that must have pushed her to such an extreme state of rebellion and suicidal despair. They also reveal, from our perspective, the lack of understanding from those charged with her care. For example, "Emma's behaviours include the abuse of drugs and alcohol, an attempted suicide . . . a rape and involvement in the taping of pornographic pictures." The suggestion is that this child is responsible for being raped and abused in pornography. In many of the diary entries, Emma is pleading for someone to understand her.

The diary entries themselves provide a fascinating insight into the mind of a very disturbed teenage girl, trying to make some sense of the mad world around her and her own troubled interior. They become particularly fascinating and powerful when Emma writes in the third person, as "Emma's friend". We know that a common psychological reaction to experiences of trauma and abuse is 'dissociation'. This is a mechanism that many victims of abuse use to protect themselves from the pain and hurt associated with the traumatic incident and/or memories of that incident, by disconnecting or separating their mind from the experience or memory. The diary entries from around November and December 1983 seem to indicate this dissociation in practice, and one entry in particular suggests a possible key traumatising event: . . .

> she saw Denni and the old photographer. She almost flipped it was all so emotional, so she left and walked towards the door. In a way she knew where she was going, but all she knew is she had to get out of there. Just seeing a part of her past, that she is trying to put away, was hard.

She came back to the centre and Jim and her had a talk. She was gone, but she'd come back once in a while. Jim was making a big deal about it, and if he hadn't of, she might have been back right now. She told him her past was her problem and when he mentioned porno, she left.

The diary entries continue when Emma first comes to England. Her hopes that living with her natural father and her new family would provide a solution to all her problems became quickly dashed. The diaries go on to provide a fascinating contemporaneous record of Emma's 'decision' to become a street prostitute, of her commencing the relationship with Trevor, of her growing fear of his violence, and eventual disintegration into an alcohol-induced oblivion. Had her lawyer had access to some of these entries at the time of the trial, or even at the appeal, they could have provided important evidence to assist her defence to murder.

Psychological Assessment
February 15th 1982
Relevant Family History
Emma reports little family problems until approximately three years ago when her mother married her current husband, Mr Al Somerville.

Until then the girl felt very close to her mother and considered herself mom's favourite. Mr Somerville appears initially to have developed [an] alliance with Emma. Emma has come to believe that her mother no longer wants her, that she has been merely useful to the woman as a maid and babysitter.

Feeling extremely bitter over this state of affairs the girl has become increasingly rebellious. She has also taken great pleasure in shocking her sister and her mother with her rebellious behaviour, especially her sexual exploits.

Personal Description
The most striking features of this adolescent are her

extreme rebelliousness, disdain for authority and cultivation of a negative identity.

Summary and Recommendations

Emma is manifesting with an intense form of adolescent rebellion and what appears to be a serious problem in identity formation.

She is cultivating a considerable negative identity in large part as a reaction to the deterioration in the relationship with her mother.

First Diary entry

Westfield
December 5th 1982
9.40pm

Dear Diary,
Well today wasn't such a bad day. I didn't do much. Kevin phoned today, the staff forgot that I was on grounded and let me talk to him. The reason why he was mad was because on the annual report it said that I had slept with someone, and it wasn't him because I didn't go that far with him when I was on AWOL, because he knows I have the infection and I will give it to him. But I wanted it so bad on Sunday I just used some guy and I guess I gave him the infection, but I told him, and also my fucking mother told him, to break up with me because I would ruin his life, like I have ruined everyone else's, and all I want out of life is to be a prostitute.

So all that got him really upset.

Emma

Emma was seen on December 8ᵗʰ 1982 at Unit 2, Westfield diagnostic and treatment centre. The following is extracted from the psychological assessment:

Psychological Report
Apparently she has been covering up for the disruptions and difficulties during the weekend visits at home as she felt that this would jeopardise her return.

This situation has been becoming increasingly severe as far as emotional abuse for Emma is concerned. The clear message from the mother is that she could not return home, and that the whole marriage situation and the other children's difficulties as well as Mrs Somerville's own emotional problems is all Emma's fault.

Mrs Sommerville also contacted Emma's boyfriend, Kevin Markwart, and informed him in no uncertain terms including many four-lettered descriptions that Emma was no good, that she would ruin his life like she had ruined everyone else's life. Kevin had telephoned Emma and told her that their relationship and friendship was over.

I perceive Emma as having a very low self-concept, she has at this point almost totally incorporated the mother's messages into her own sense of worth and her own functioning.

December 9th 1982
6.20pm
Quiet Time

Dear Diary,
So the last few days have been the pits. I AWOLed on Tuesday at about twelve just before lunch. I went with Darlene and Tracey, I got picked up at about seven in Edmonton Centre. The cop that brought me back, Brian, was real nice, but his partner was a real bastard and called me a two-bit hooker.

When I came back I was kinda depressed and went to the bathroom and went rank on my arms. Fay caught me and I was feeling kinda faint and I was really shaky and cold.

Joey took me to the hospital. I didn't need any stitches but they wanted me to take some pills to take me out of depression, but I refused to take them.

Psychological Report
January 5th 1983
This has not been one of the most positive weeks for this girl as she has reported that she arranged a family meeting, had contacted her mother and found that she was drunk, but she had gone with her volunteer to deliver some cookies for the younger children.

The mother was careering around the room screaming obscenities and generally being very unpleasant.

The two young boys had been left at the Bisel Centre, one of the sisters had gone to pick them up and Emma and the volunteer were concerned that the children would not be properly cared for.

The stepfather was there in the home as well and apparently he was intoxicated as well.

January 6th 1983
9.45pm

Dear Diary,
Oh Fuck! I am in love again, he's just what I am looking for – 22, single, house, I'm not joking a fucking limo, continental, cab city, fur coats and a photographer and model.

We met him at Kingsway bus stop.

His name is Rob. Sandy blond oh fuck I hope he's mine.

Me, Sherrie and Rose met him today 'cause we went downtown shopping.

Emma

January 12th 1983

Today I ran away from Westfield unit with Susan Sawyers.
We'd planned it for a long time.

Emma

March 1983

My name is Emma Humphreys. I live at Westfield on the
west end of Edmonton. I am now in the psychiatric ward of
the general hospital.

I had run away that day, I ran home. When the police
came to pick me up I locked myself into the bathroom and
cut my wrists, they took me in an ambulance to the
University Hospital of Alberta. I was then transferred to this
hospital.

Dr Blashko wants to move me out pretty soon, but I don't
think I am ready to move yet because I still think of suicide as
the best way out.

Sometimes I wish I was dead. If there was a bottle of pills
here and a razor blade I think I would do away with myself.

I am going down to legal aid with Brenda from Westfield
today. I want to take it to court to see if they will let me go
home and live with my mom. I think I have a good chance of
winning.

Emma Clare Humphreys

March 6th 1983
20.50
General Hospital, room 35

Dear Diary,
Well, I don't think I am doing too good. I came to the
hospital on Wednesday morning. First they put me in the
lock up ward, but now I'm in the open ward.

Al has taken the kids down to Calgary, without mom's
permission so mom is going to go to court to get temporary
custody of both of the boys until there can be a final hearing.

Mom is in real bad shape, she is drinking twenty-four hours a day and she isn't eating and is down to 98lbs. I am not allowed contact with mom for a while, because she upsets me. Her, Darryl, Rebecca and Abigail came to visit me today and Debbie took me out for Chinese food.

Brain and Lori came to see me yesterday, but I haven't heard from Susan for a while.

The reason I am here is because I slashed my wrists again.

Emma Humphreys

March 9th 1983
4.12pm
Unit 3 Westfield

Dear Diary,
Well, I am back in unit three again and I want to die. They have cut off all contact with my mom, fuck, that pisses me off. I jabbed a piece of glass into my arms this morning. I wanted to talk to August, so he is on his way over. I am going to try to con him into some things. I have tried to sneak a phone call to my mom today, but that fucking bitch staff hung up the phone.

Also I went rank on my social worker at the hospital today, so the security guards had to come up and restrain me.

Emma Humphreys

Dear Diary,
Well, I'm not dead yet, I talked to August earlier today, so I think that I'm going to give this hole a shot. I just decided that if I keep smiling and kiss ass all the time I will probably be off C.S. [Close Supervision] by the weekend. Mardon Michelle phoned Dr Blashko this afternoon and now I have to take more pills.

That's all,

Emma Humphreys

Same day but 9.00pm

Dear Diary,
Well, I feel like I have murdered someone, they treat me like shit. I wish that someone would just understand. I had my nightmare again last night, it really freaks me out.

Emma Humphreys

Memo
Received on March 18th 1983
From Don Clifford Program Supervisor Unit 3
To John Taylor Assistant Director, Westfield

While AWOL Emma's behaviours include the abuse of drugs and alcohol, an attempted suicide, (superficial cuts were noted upon re-admission February 28th 1983), a rape and involvement in the taping of pornographic pictures.

Psychological Report
She has slashed her wrists seriously earlier in the morning and had to be taken to the hospital.

Her mood and affect during the interview was extremely flat. Emma was not hostile with me but was so towards residential staff, stating that no one understands her.

She feels that she has worked diligently for nine months to go home and there is absolutely no use in her doing so since the home situation is so chaotic.

The unit 3 staff perceive Emma as a real danger to herself as I do. She was left alone for between one and two minutes this morning and managed to obtain a cosmetics jar which she smashed, and slashed her wrists.

This report was by A.E. Swindlehurst, Consulting Psychologist.

April 25th 1983
6.30pm

Dear Diary,
I am so happy my dad phoned today all the way from good old England, I didn't get to talk to him, but he is phoning tomorrow at 3.00pm so I will get to talk to him then.
    I haven't talked to him for almost five years.

Love Emma Clare Humphreys

May 17th 1983

Dear Diary,
It is about 9.30pm . . . I wish I were dead.
    I really do not want to live any more. I am going to kill myself . . .
    My plan is to break my glass pepsi bottle and slice my wrists.
    I WANT TO DIE . . .
    PLEASE LET ME DIE THIS TIME . . .

Emma Clare Humphreys

May 17th 1983

Dear Diary,
I wish I had a bottle of pills and a razor blade cause I really feel suicidal . . . DEATH . . . Emma wants to sleep for ever . . .
    Emma can't take much more of life . . . Emma wishes she were DEAD . . .
    I am getting so fat but I can't stop eating.

Emma Clare Humphreys

July 24th 1983
10.15pm

Why couldn't I have died when I slashed my wrists?
Who the hell wants me to live?
Why can't I die if I want to?
Why are there never any answers?

I am sure that even if I live and go back to England to live with my dad, by the time I am 21 I will have been and done everything I have ever wanted to do. And it will be up to me by that time. I think I will be so lonely, bored and angry that I will take my own life.

Am I different than normal people, am I going to end up a schizophrenic, a murderer, a drug addict . . . am I going to live my whole life in institutions and hospitals or will I some day find someone who really cares about me and start a family of my own? Or will my life repeat over again with my husband and I will be in my mom's shoes next time? Should I really keep living, what am I going to find?

Emma

Family/Community Situation

Emma has two sisters and two step-brothers. Her mother, Pamela June Sommerville, entered Canada about five years ago and is currently involved in deportation proceedings.

Emma's father John Humphreys remained in Britain and has since remarried. He has stated his intention to assume responsibility for Emma and has been working towards that end.

Mr and Mrs Sommerville are presently separated and there are numerous reports on the file of problem drinking, abuse and neglect of the children. All three girls have been apprehended at one time or another.

Emma has made numerous suicide attempts and has been hospitalised twice.

By her own admission Emma has been involved in child pornography, promiscuity, alcohol and drug abuse. Her numerous suicide attempts will continue to be of great concern.

September 7th 1983
6.00pm
Y.D.C.

Dear Diary,
Well, everyone knows that I want to go back to England to live with my dad and his family and start a new life. I don't think it is going to be all roses, but the problems that we will run into will be discussed instead of me taking off again. It's different than every other time I have been locked up. I used to put on a big play and say I wouldn't run away anymore, and all along in my mind I would just be saying what a bunch of suckers.

I think it was because I could see no future for myself, just drugs, people taking advantage of me and probably ending up in jail. No one has ever asked me what I think is best or what I want. Everybody else would think for me and do what they thought was best, and that isn't always the best thing.

October 10th 1983
3.30pm

Dear Diary,
Well, it's quiet time now and I just got up from a visit with Debbie! We had a good visit. We talked about pregnancy, abortions and I.V.F. 'cause she is pregnant and due in March. Anyway, we were talking about my step dad Al and his drinking and I found out something about when I was on cascade. Abigail phoned me and asked me what is it any of the social workers' business that Al was in jail twelve years ago, and I said it isn't any of their business. And Abi said, "Well why did you tell them?" and we started arguing, and she finally hung up cause I said I didn't know that he was in jail.

Anyway, I asked Debbie if she knew any thing about him being in jail and she said yes. That once mom had gone down to pick up the kids when Al had kidnapped them, the police that went in to get them said that Al had a very bad criminal record. So when mom came back and was drunk and phoned Debbie, she told Debbie that about two years ago Al was charged with attempted murder and assault. So that's pretty fucking wild.

Emma

Same day

I never had a mother to daughter relationship with my mom. I remember when I started my periods I told my mom and she sent me to my older sister, and when I was having trouble with my ovaries and fallopian tubes and I was in hospital to have it straightened out, I told my mom I was told I may never be able to have kids of my own. She said that was better for me because I would probably end up being knocked up twenty times before I was nineteen. That really made me feel good!

Emma

October 17th 1983
10.00pm

Dear Diary,
At 9.00 Irene came to talk to me and said that mom phoned and said she doesn't want me phoning anymore and swearing and saying negative things to the family. That's all bullshit 'cause all I said to the boys was I missed them and they started to cry and saying that they wanted me to come home, and that's all.

Emma

November 7th 1983
7.15pm

Dear Diary,
Well, I got a visit today from the consultant that is doing the home study on mom's place in Edmonton and Al's place in Calgary, 'cause there is a custody battle going on.

So I guess he's been around to mom's and Al's place and both of them defended themselves, only telling stuff about each other. The consultant knows what is going on.

So I think the kids will be taken into care. I was really upset after that visit, but I know that my side of things will help get the kids out of there, and if they're out of there before I go I can have them come in and visit me.

But it will be best for them and she said that they wouldn't get split up. I can't let this all go to my head, because it has crossed my mind to kidnap them, 'cause I love them and they deserve a good life.

I sat and cried for them after my visit that lasted two and a half hours, I just can't forget them, I love them so much no one could ever understand how I feel.

I saw my dad's birthday card mail in Jim's box so I will get that tomorrow.

I did crafts for two hours last night and I wrote my dad tonight.

Love Emma

November 17th 1983
10.40pm

Dear Diary,
Emma's gone away! She's cold, lonely and ready to give up on life. She had a meeting with Glen, Loopee, Ken, Cye and Jean.

She's upset, shaking with coldness, wants to die, wants warmth.

She's falling apart because of all of the suspense, she thinks people are going to lock her away where people don't care.

She's old and baggy looking, putting on weight. She wants
space. Six weeks till Christmas, that makes her scared, how
could her passport be ready in six weeks?

Why is she throwing it all away? Don't let them win, Emma.

Come back and start to fight again. It's a long hard game
but you can do it, don't give in. There is always a winner and
a loser.

She feels dirty.

Emma's crazy, Emma's crazy, Emma's crazy, Emma's crazy,
Emma's crazy, Emma's Crazy,

No! Emma needs security, reassurance, space, warmth and
love.

She keeps coming back but she slips away, right away.

Emma's Friend

November 27th 1983
7.58pm

Dear Diary,
I'm so frustrated I feel like I'm going to blow. I have been
holding it in for a couple of days now, and pretty soon I am
going to flip on someone else or on myself.

I need space, I need to get away, anywhere, somewhere
alone and lonely and quiet.

Please will someone listen to me, can't you see what's
happening to me?

I need space, lots of it. I don't want to die and I don't want
to live. There has to be something.

All alone in my own world. No light, no noise, no food.
Somebody listen, please.

I hate people, it's like an ache going through my body when
I think of people. I love so many people. And I hate so many
people – no, I don't hate people. I hate things – they are
people, but I don't even know what it is that I hate, it's the
physical part of people.

I'm no good.

Emma has gone now. She got too upset, she couldn't

handle it, it was all too much for her. She tries to explain things, but doesn't know what it is. Doesn't anybody care or understand or even notice that she needs something?

She is so confused about life and her future. I think that she's scared of leaving to go to her dad's, she's been hurt so many times before and she doesn't want to hurt any more people.

She is back.

I went, but my friend said a lot that I needed to put down, but it was too hard, too straining and too much pressure.

I feel better now I am back.

Emma

November 27th 1983
9.30pm

Crazy crazy crazy crazi

die die die die die die die die
die die die die die die die
die die die die die die die die
die die die die die die die die
die die die die die die die
blood blood blood blood
blood blood blood blood
blood blood blood blood
blood blood blood blood
blood blood blood blood
blood blood blood blood
blood blood blood blood
blood blood blood blood blood
blood blood blood blood blood
blood blood blood blood blood
She's gone, please come back.
die, die, die die die die die die die
die, die, die die die die die die die
die, die, die die die die die die die

die, die, die die die die die die die
die, die, die die die die die die die
die, die, die die die die die die die
die, die, die die die die die die die
die, die, die die die die die die die
die die Emma give up. die
die, die, die die die die die die die
die, die, die die die die die die die
die, die, die die die die die die die
die, die, die die die die die die die
die, die, die die die die die die die
die, die, die die die die die die die
die, die, die die die die die die die
die, die, die die die die die die die
die, die, die die die die die die die
come back or stay away die
die, die, die die die die die gone die
die, can't die die die die die die
die die die die die die die die die
die die die die die die die die die
die die die die die die die die die
die die, die die die die die die die
die dig half die die die die die die
die die die die die die die die die
die die die die die die die die die
die die die die die die die die die
die die die die die die dead soon
die die die die die die die die die
die die die die die die die die die
die die die die die die die die die
die die, die die die die die die die
die die die die die die die die die
die die die die die die die die die
die die die die die die die die die
die die, die die die die die hide
dark die die die die die die die die die
die go die die die die die die die die

die die die die die die die die die
die die, die die die die die die die
die die die die die die die die die
die die die die die die die die die
die die, die die die die die die die
don't know aches hurt sleep
forewarn life no don't cant try
stop no no I cant talk cant
why why why why why why why
why why why why why why why why
why why why why why why why
why why why why why why why why why
why why why why why why why why
why why why why why why why why
why why why why why why why
why why why why they're gonna get
me. why why why why why why why

Emma

December 3rd 1983
10.05pm

Dear Diary,
Emma's gone away, shit did her mind flip. I was worried about her, fuck I thought it was over for her.

She was trying and she did come back for a couple of minutes, a couple of times, but shit she almost stayed and ended it all, but she's taking a break and I think that's the best thing.

She went out shopping with Debbie…

She was happy about that and was having a good time, but she saw Denni and the old photographer. She almost flipped it was all so emotional, so she left and walked towards the door. In a way she knew where she was going, but all she knew is she had to get out of there. Just seeing a part of her past, that she is trying to put away, was hard.

She came back to the centre and Jim and her had a talk.
She was gone, but she'd come back once in a while. Jim was
making a big deal about it, and if he hadn't of, she might have
been back right now. She told him her past was her problem,
and when he mentioned porno, she left. But the
communication was awful, she was trying to come back.

Jim was saying she is putting herself on a guilt trip. I sure
wish there was someone apart from these shit heads that
think that they do understand her . . . why am I the only one
who understands her?

She left this time cause she got really paranoid. How did
Jim know that this had anything to do with pornography?

Jesus, her goddamn past always does this to her. She wants
to come back and forget it, but it was the way their eyes
met, it was so emotional she wanted to run far, far away.

She was trying not to leave, but now it's like anything and
everything that upsets her. She just leaves now.

Emma's Friend

December 3rd 1983
10.30pm

Dear Diary,
I feel like shit, I had to leave it was so awful. The way our
eyes met I thought I was "on" right at that moment, and had
to get away.

It was just like I was on the set, I had to get away, but I
tried to get back sooner, but I couldn't.

I embarrassed myself and I really do feel like a piece of shit.

I really felt like ending it and I was so alone tonight.

Emma

December 4th 1983
7.00pm

Dear Diary,
I feel like I want to hide in a small dark room and kill myself.
I feel really paranoid of people.

I feel myself trying to leave again, to get away from
everything, 'cause sometimes when I leave for a while and
then come back I feel better.

I feel like suicide but my future is holding me back. I know I
can't change everything from my past, but I can change or
make sure I get a future. It's awful not being able to talk to
people and tell them how I feel. Maybe that's why I'm
starting to leave so much more. I feel like I need help, but I
won't go for help here 'cause then I would have no future,
cause any talk about suicide and I will have no future. I know
that for a fact.

So as soon as I get over there, if I don't feel any better and
I still have the same kind of feelings, I will get some help and
start looking for some more professional help, 'cause I hate
myself right now because of the way I am feeling.

Dr Blashko always told me to tell someone when I have
these thoughts, but it could only destroy my future.

I really need to talk to someone, why is it that I feel this way?

Emma
Talk to you later.

Emma arrives in Nottingham – she is staying at her dad's home with his wife, Elizabeth and their children, Rachel and John.

January 10th 1984
1.30pm
Home

Dear Diary,
I don't know what to say. First off I want to apologise for not writing since the first of the month . . .

I don't know if I am coming or going. I honestly don't feel like trying any more. I have a feeling that I am letting a lot of people down by not being happy or enthusiastic about anything . . . I expected to have a great time over here, remembering things from before I left, but it's like nothing ever happened in the first ten years of my life.

One thing I can remember very clearly is when we were living on Cotton Hill with Bill, the night my mom tried to commit suicide. That is something that I have always remembered about my past, and it is the worst thing in my past in England.

I don't feel like the same person anymore. I have no interests or enthusiasm for any thing, I feel I am wasting my time going on.

The weird thing is that whenever I think of suicide I always think of my past in Canada and what it was like for me over there.

I think that instead of Adam, Simon, mom, Rebecca, Abigail and myself going through all of this agony, we should kill ourselves all together in a room that we all knew and we could die all together. It wouldn't have to be a messy or painful death for us all, we could just take too many pills and end it all, but we would be together, that's what I think is one of the best answers.

Not one of the people listed above are happy with life, not one of us six, and I just think that we have gone through enough mental pain.

Emma

January 12th 1984
10.30pm
Home

Dear Diary,
I don't know why I am not writing regularly now, but when I think about writing I put it off, you know? I think I know why, because I like to tell you exactly how I feel. I think I'm not writing because I am trying to avoid the way I really feel about things. Because I really feel like this was not what I wanted or expected. And by admitting that I feel like this, I will hurt a lot of people and let them down, and it makes me feel bad, guilty and ungrateful.

Let me explain . . . it's not my family or the home, it's me.

I've got a wonderful family here but I'm not happy, I feel so ashamed and ungrateful.

I have no feelings for the family, like I said, and it's true. If they all dropped dead in front of me I wouldn't feel anything.

When I was back in Y.D.C. [Youth Detention Centre] I was working for something, to come home and that kept me on the ball. Now it seems like there is nothing to work for, nothing to live for.

Well, excuse me for a minute, I'm gonna hit the bottle and get a drink.

Emma

Emma has moved out from her dad's home, having clashed badly with Elizabeth. She is now living with 'Nana' – her mum's mother, also in Nottingham.

March 26th 1984
9.15pm (approx.)
same place

Dear Diary,
Mom phoned at 7.00 am . . . she asked what happened at dad's, so I told her the story briefly and she said she and I know she would do anything for us.

And Mom, do you remember the time when you put myself, Abigail and Rebecca into a taxi, kissed us all goodbye, so you could take an overdose and slash your wrists?

Mom, so clearly now I can see you standing at that cab door, you were sending us to Nana's, and on the way to Nana's I can remember a corner of a street we drove through. It's there in my mind.

But I don't know why, what's happened to us all mom? Why?

Mom, my greatest fear is of you dying.

My diary knows that too. Because I have decided just a while ago that when you die I am going too.

Mom.

In the future I think I see you committing suicide, but please mom take me, Adam, Simon, Rebecca, and Abigail with you please.

Good night mom.

I'm too upset to write any further.

Emma

Same place
April 3rd 1984
11.55pm

Dear Diary,

My Own World
I live in my own world
away from others . . .
who do not understand the mental pain,
that is inside of myself
so unknown by Emma.
We, it or Emma, or myself
Who? I don't know
is very scared to wake up
to sleep
to live
I am scared
to find some more
pain inside
the rusty object
that holds the pain.
be it my heart,
please take it
and my soul
recycle it
and let me loose
from my own world

Emma

Friday May 4th 1984
9.27pm
Same place

Dear Diary,
I got up at around 8.15. When mom phoned I had a few words with her, and she told me, "don't ever come to my house, the only way I want to see you is dead." How's that for the beginning of a day?

I sometimes try to kid myself that it doesn't hurt, but it does, it hurts every part of me.

Emma

Emma was very unhappy being back in England, and thought that the best thing was to return to Canada. Her Nana and dad contributed to the price of her return ticket, but when she arrived in Canada, immigration control would not allow her to re-enter the country. She was allowed to stay overnight with one of her foster mothers, but from there went on the run for several weeks, before picked up by the police and placed on a plane back to England. She returned to Nottingham to stay with her grandmother.

June 26th 1984
Seattle

Dear Diary,
Well, how the fuck are you? As for me, well, I really missed you. By looking at the date since the last time I wrote it has been quite a while, but I really missed you. Before I start my long interesting story, I will tell you that you have been sitting in my suitcase in the holding cell in the immigration department of Edmonton international airport for the last forty-nine days, and right now I am writing to you from the inside of a British Airways Boeing 747 aeroplane.

We are on the ground at the airport in Seattle, waiting for our return flight to London, England.

July 23rd 1984
7.30

Dear Diary:

Full Memories
The fullness of life gone away.
The memories of hard earned money,
money from abuse and lost people
I want to go back
to be happy the next morning counting the filthy money,
money earned by the other Emma.
To want to own,
to have fullness of material luxuries,
But to be eaten away,
eaten up by society.
There seems no other way
to bring in the money,
To have something to call mine,
To be in control.
All of these flash backs of needs
Of what was once my life
Brought back my full memories.

Emma

July 23rd 1984
7.45pm

Dear Diary,
Well, how are you? Well, as for me I'm doing not too badly.
I'm seriously considering going back to the streets. I need the
money just so I will have to have my own place.

If I could maybe get a room for the nights.

I'd need some clothes to start off with, but after that I'll be
able to buy all the clothes that I want to, I'll be able to buy
what I want.

So tonight I'm going to phone dad and ask him right out for
twenty or twenty five pounds to buy some clothes.

I know I can make it again and it's a point of having to.
I need to be in control again.

August 1st 1984
3.15pm

Dear Diary,
Well, last night when I was lying in bed I was thinking about
some of the awful things that happened with the family when
mom and Al were together. I know there were awful,
horrible and frightening things that happened when everyone
was in their states.

One time I could really remember was back about two to
two and a half years ago when we were living at 107 St, the
first house in Edmonton.

I remember Abi, Rebecca and I had been out somewhere,
and when we returned home we went into the house and all
we could hear was mom screaming, but we didn't know
where she was. We looked at Al, and could tell by his eyes
and by the booze sitting around that he was drunk. We
asked him where mom was, but he wouldn't answer us so
we went looking around the house. We finally found my
mom sitting in the corner of the cold, black, storage room.

Al had beaten her up and then put her in there and shut
the door, and mom had been too scared to move.

I can't remember what happened after we found her, but I
remember that mom was half drunk too.

It makes me cold and upset when I think of times like that.

Love Emma

August 2 1984
3.17pm
Same place

Dear Diary,
Well, we had all gone to bed when the phone rang at 12.00.
I answered it and it was my mom.
   This was the conversation:
      Mom: Oh it's you bitch, where is your Nana?
      Emma: I beg your pardon?
      Mom: Where's your Nana?
      Emma: In bed sleeping.
      Mom: At this time of day?
      Emma: Yes, it's night time over here, that's when people
      go to bed and sleep,
      Mom: Oh don't give me that Canadian accent, you fat
      bitch.
      Emma: Laughed
      Mom: Hung up
   When I laughed at her she got mad and hung up, she was
very drunk and it's only four in the afternoon over there.
   God I feel sorry for the little boys, well there isn't much I
can do.

August 20th 1984
2.00pm

Dear Diary,
How are you? Well, I hope you are better than I am. God,
I just don't know what to do with myself.
   Nana and I aren't talking again. Fuck, I wish she would just
quit feeling sorry for herself and being so judgemental
towards me.
   She spends all day putting words in my mouth. If she says
anything to irritate me today I am gonna blow up. 'Cause I'm
sick of it, I really am.
   I don't know whether to just pack up my things and go. I

don't know where to. Maybe London, anywhere, I just don't know. Fuck, I wish I knew what to do.

Emma

August 27th 1984
1.15pm

Dear Diary,
There were times when I laughed.
There were times when I cried of fear.
But one time I cried for joy.
That was the day when I moved to
Westfield and my mom was there, I hadn't seen her in two months, I hugged her and cried for joy.
Rebecca was there, so was Adam and Simon, but Abigail wasn't there because she was in a foster home after Al tried to strangle her.

Emma

August 31st 1984
10.50am
Jane's

Dear Diary,
Well, I finally walked out of Nana's, but god how I would love to go back. I'm just staying with a girl I met. I'll write more later.

Emma

September 1st 1984
2.25pm
Jane's

Dear Diary,
Well here I am in a stinky absolutely filthy house, oh it's so grossly filthy you would have to see it to believe me, but it's a roof over my head.

Well, last night I was going to stay at the Y.M.C.A., but it was closed, so I had to go stay in a hotel. I had a good clean night's sleep but now I have no money left, so I had to come and stay here until Monday, when I try to find a place then go and get my rent paid.

Or else I'm going to have to live here until Saturday next week when I get my giro.

But I hope I can find a place on Monday. I hope to find a place somewhere near Forest Road, 'cause I am gonna work the streets until I get settled with everything I need again.

I phoned dad again yesterday but Elizabeth answered the phone, and when I asked if he was there she said, "No, he isn't, and don't bother phoning back again." But I'm going to phone back at about 9.30 or 10.00 tonight, 'cause I need some more money just to keep me going.

I just feel filthy and dirty, I can't wait to get out of here. I can't even make myself some soup or anything 'cause it's so dirty. It makes me really sick to my stomach, and the smell, oh it's gross.

Will talk, write to you later.

Love Emma.

September 10th 1984
1.20pm

Dear Diary,
Well, how the fuck are you doing? As for me, well, I'm back working the streets on Forest Road every night.

I'm moving out of Jane's tonight and moving into Trevor's pub. Trevor was one of my tricks, but now I go to his pub every night.

I've lost some more weight, but I'm not trying to. It's fucking cold outside, standing there for a couple of hours. I feel really fucked, 'cause I've been getting pissed every night. I've had no problem with the cops out there. I get a lot of compliments from everyone 'cause of my legs.

Love Emma

September 25th 1984
3.07pm
Trevor's

Dear Diary,
Well anyway, I better tell you what's happening with me. About a week ago I moved in with Trevor. I'm happy staying here, but I'm drinking all day. But it helps to make work a little better when I' m pissed.

I met another guy. I call him the reindeer man, 'cause he lived in Alberta for quite a few years. So most nights in the middle of working I go down to the pub for a drink with him.

Dad phoned me last week, he just wanted to know if I was alright and asked me what I wanted for my birthday. He's phoning again this week. Yes, I'm seventeen in thirty-five days, god I don't want to grow up 'cause it scares me. I want to stay young.

I think Trevor is sick of me already. Every time I fuck I get a brownie coloured discharge, but I'm scared to go to the doctors in case it's something I don't want. So at work I just do oral even though I hate it.

I had a guy last night that didn't pay. Trevor doesn't believe me, that bothers me. I was shitting my pants cause we were in the middle of a cabbage field and he was real mad.

Well I'm gonna go

Love Emma.

October 22nd 1984
Same place

Dear Diary,
Well, I'm sorry I haven't written for a while but God I'm so scared, please help me, please I'm so scared, I'm gonna do it but I don't want to, please help me, god.

I've never lied to him, ever, but why does he do this, why? I can't put up with it anymore, he hurts me and I don't know why, I try to be good to him, I am good to him, he never thinks I'm working, but I do, at least I try.

God, I wish you would help me to end it all, can't you see what a mess it is? Everything what I am doing to myself. I wish you could talk back to me. Sometimes, like now, I need someone to talk to, but I'm gonna tell you what happened tonight.

I came home from shopping and Trevor was at home from work. I was in a good mood cause I'd finally paid for the ring I wanted.

I don't know, maybe he thought I'd been out with someone else, but I hadn't, so he left and said he would be back in half an hour, but he wasn't.

Still in the meantime a guy (I won't put his name) phoned and wanted three whores for nine o'clock, so I really didn't know what to do, so I took a taxi down to work and tried for about half an hour to look for some decent whores to take.

There wasn't any, not even ugly . . . So I came home and then I decided to give it another try, so I went back out in a taxi and found two. But when I got home Trevor wasn't home and hadn't been home, so I left him a note 'cause I wasn't going to go on an all-nighter until he said yes. So when they phoned I said "I can't go but I've got two others", but they said no. So I had to phone the two others (I won't say their names) and tell them it was off.

So then I took another taxi back to work and did two and came home.

But Trevor is mad at me. He doesn't know what I did tonight, but I'm gonna go ask him if I can do a four-hour tomorrow night, cause they came round again later when I was working.

It's better than standing out there and freezing, so I hope I can do that tomorrow night.

I don't know what he thinks I do? I stand out there or lie on my back while he is thinking I'm doing things, he's doing sweet fuck all.

He wonders why I get mad when he goes out and I don't know where he's been. I've never been in bed with another guy since I met Trevor.

Love Emma
P.S. I Love You (sparrow legs)

October 25th 1984
9.45pm
Same place

Dear Diary,
Well, here I am again. I feel in the same state of mind, my god what a hell of a couple of hours. I just don't know what to say, I'm stunned for words.

He's trying to convince me that I'm wrong he's calling me a liar. I'm scared to death again he is convincing me that I'm lying, my god, everything worked out perfectly for him to hit me.

Something either wants me dead or out of this house, but I don't want to go and I don't think Trevor wants me to leave, but god how the past two hours have worked in his favour to hit me.

God how I just want to pack everything and go, because I don't want to be beat anymore and god how I'd do anything to have the guts to kill myself, maybe if I sat here and drank the rest of the bottle I'll do it, I just don't know.

Talk to you later

Love Emma

October 30th 1984
2.00pm
Same place [Emma's 17th birthday]

Dear Diary,
Well, here I am in the same state again, it seems to be becoming a regular thing. Jesus Christ, why the hell don't you talk back to me?

Well, I was physically OK until about an hour ago, but I wasn't mentally OK, but now I'm fucked up to the roots of my hair. If this headache doesn't go away I'll drive a knife through it, why does he always hit me?

I told you before that I didn't think I could take any more, but now it's getting worse, and the awful thing is that afterwards I get convinced that it's all my fault, but no, I know it isn't.

He doesn't have the right to do it to me, so why? You tell me.

Anyways, business the last two nights has been the shits.

Yesterday's gone, today is here, tomorrow is?

Love Emma

November 17th 1984
(approx 1.00pm)
Cantock Hotel

Dear Diary,
Well, here I am again and it's been a while again, and quite a lot has happened.

First of all I left Trevor yesterday, and this time I am not going back. I just got so fed up of his jealousy and ugliness and he was always hitting me.

So I decided enough is enough. So I am staying in a hotel until I can find myself a flat and stuff.

Well, I met another guy, his name is Anthony, but it seems like he just wants to pimp me and buy a car and go running around which is not what I want to do. So we will see what happens when he comes back from London.

I'm working pretty hard to send lots of stuff for the family at Christmas. I've already got quite a bit, I went and dropped it off at Nana's yesterday so it wouldn't get thrown around and stuff. I only stayed and chatted for a couple of minutes 'cause I was on my way to work.

On the night of my birthday I went to stay in a hotel, because the night before Trevor had given me a black eye and I didn't feel like getting another beating over nothing.

But I guess my mom phoned for me that night and gave Trevor her phone number but I would never have had it, because he had it in his trouser pocket and I don't think he had any intention of giving it to me.

I found it while snooping through his suit one day.

Anyways, I got picked up by the law a couple of weeks ago and got a caution for soliciting and loitering, I got another caution then a fifty pound fine which I guess isn't too bad.

I also got raped at scissor point by three deaf and dumb Black men. I couldn't report it because I went into the flat willingly, supposedly for business. Then last week I got taken down to the police station and questioned for a couple of hours, twice about a Black guy who I was supposed to have known who stabbed and robbed a shop keeper on the opposite side of the street to where I work.

Well, that's the only boring wonderful news I have for you lately.

Love Emma

December 1st 1984
approx 1.35pm
Cantock Hotel

Dear Diary,
Hello, how are you? Well, I guess I'm not doing too badly. I'm still at the hotel and working every night.

Well, I've had no more hassle from the cops. I picked up my stuff from Nana's last Saturday, and stopped for about an hour and had a cup of tea, but she told me if I come again, don't bring my Black boy friend. That stupid prejudiced fucking bitch.

Oh well, Anthony wants me to go to work up at Aberdeen for a couple of weeks, but I don't want to go 'cause I'm scared. I mean, I don't know the place.

Well we'll talk to you soon.

Love Emma

December 14th 1984
1.25pm
Astra Hotel

Dear Diary,
Well, I got kicked out of a few hotels since I last wrote, and Anthony has left me but I don't know why.

I'm still working every night, but I got picked up two nights ago for the third time so I have to go to court on January 17th for a fine, I think. I will get locked up if I get picked up before court.

Love Emma

January 3rd 1985
4.15pm
Southwell House

Dear Diary,
Hello, well here I am, pissed again.

A lot has happened since I last wrote, I don't know where to start.

Well, I went back to Trevor for one night, then the next night Toni came over – Fuck this, I'll tell you in a short time.

First of all, Toni and I got put in Hucknall cells for a couple of days 'cause I smashed up Trevor's house. Then I got out on bail.

Toni had no charges, 'cause I'd done it all.

Then I haven't seen Toni since about four days after I went to court.

So Xmas day Vicki and Franklyn came to the Peeham hotel. But in the end I assaulted the hotel manager and a police officer and ended up at Radford Road cells for a couple of days until court. I got out on bail.

And I'm in a hostel until I go to court on the 17th January. Hopefully I can come back to the hotel cause I don't want to go to prison.

Talk later

Love Emma

Saturday January 19th 1985
approx 10.00am
Same place

Dear Diary,
Well, how the fuck are you? Well, as for me I'm still here and not in Risley. I went to court on Thursday and pleaded guilty to the four charges, so I got bailed back to here for five weeks until I go to court on February 21st 1985. But I don't know what will happen then, because in the beginning I was hoping to spend a year here, but because of my behaviour

the hostel don't want me back here after the five weeks. Yesterday I decided to try hard to kick the drink, so I haven't bought a bottle since the day before court, but I feel so fucked up.

Love you and leave you

Love Emma

That was the last but one diary entry. We know that Emma had been arrested for the criminal damage to Trevor's flat, and then further arrested for assaulting a hotel manager. She was bailed to a probation hostel, but breached her bail and therefore was remanded into custody at Risley prison. On 21 February she was released into Trevor Armitage's 'care'. She was arrested for his murder four days later, on February 25 1985.

Dr Michael Tarsh, the psychiatric expert instructed by Emma's defence solicitor, wrote:

> It is clear both from her history and from examination that this a girl of abnormal personality with immature and explosive and attention seeking traits. She has had frequent mood swings and I would agree that she is an abnormal girl . . .

Mother

I miss you being in my life.
I miss not knowing how you are.

I love you for who you are.
I love you like I love no other.

I live to love you.
I live for you to love me.

You never leave my thoughts.
You never leave my heart.

You . . . Mother.

June 1st 1994

Escape

For just one moment
Help me to escape this body.

I ask for nothing more
And I shall never ask again.

For behind this exterior
Lies a tormented, confused woman.

Holding on with all her might
To the mould of her shackled child-self.

Help me step out to observe and find
The unsolved puzzle of my conditioning.

I'm desperate to find the solution
But it's too hard from inside this troubled body.

Please help me to escape.

July 1994
Holloway

Emma aged sixteen, 1983.

2: Telling My Story

The following story was written by Emma over a few months in 1988, less than three years after being convicted in December 1985 of murdering Trevor Armitage. At the time Emma was in Durham prison, a high-security jail for women, where she had been since she was 17 years old. Emma described entering her cell in Durham as 'walking into a coffin'. She was housed in a wing with convicted IRA terrorists, and many others who were considered a serious danger to the public. Nothing much is known about Emma's state of mind before she began to write, although we do know that she abandoned her right to appeal some months after her conviction. However, we can assume that the first three years would have been spent in shock and guilt.

Once Emma was able to face the reality of her situation, she obviously saw writing her story as a way to make sense of and understand what led up to it. Perhaps she was encouraged to do so by a prison officer or counselor or one of the other women. Or maybe the motivation came from within, in the same way as it did when she wrote her diaries about her earlier life when she was in children's homes. Either way, something compelled Emma to tell her story, long before she contacted Justice for Women for help in challenging her murder conviction.

Emma's analysis of her situation with Armitage is somewhat different to that made some years later. In the following account

of the significant factors in the build-up to the killing, in particular her descriptions of prostitution and abuse, and the violent
and possessive tendencies of Armitage, she seems to be
attempting to excuse men and blame herself – a common coping
mechanism used by many abused children and women. Emma
seems to be searching for remorse and seeking forgiveness,
rather than looking at the ways in which she was provoked into
killing as a result of men's abuse.

Her approach changed in later years, during her final phase
in prison, and in the three years after her release and before
her death, where she developed a fairly sophisticated feminist
analysis of her situation and of Armitage's complicity in his own
death. For example, in the story below, Emma describes being
abused into pornography as a child by saying: "I got myself into
a situation where pornographic photos were taken of me,"
whereas some years later she described that same scenario to
a friend, and used the words "forced" and "coerced" to explain
how it had happened.

Similarly, Emma writes about meeting a man called 'Toni' on
the beat, and insists that he wants to get her out of prostitution. However, when she was writing her diary, recording feelings and events close to the actual time they occurred, she said
this of Toni (aka Anthony): "Well, I met another guy, his name
is Anthony, but it seems like he just wants to pimp me and buy
a car . . ."

It is with these factors in mind that we invite you to read
Emma's unique and powerful retrospective account of the build-
up to her killing Armitage . . .

Today as I write this I would like to think I have my life totally
in order, and have quit being a rebel to myself. I don't agree
to being called a rebel to society, because I have not hurt or
upset society half as much as I have upset myself.

I am writing this book for you and other readers to
hopefully understand more about children like me. I still feel a
child inside. I am coming up to my 21st birthday, and I still
feel 13. I am still the same size as I was eight years ago,

maybe even half a stone smaller. I don't look big and hard like some people may expect me to look. I look like a typical 16 year old.

If you discussed some of the incidents with your friends before reading this book, I figure you would automatically think of me as a nasty, self-centred person. But I'm not. I am as human and thoughtful as you are. That's what I hope to help you understand: that there are thousands of children like me in the world, who somehow get lost in their teenage years and end up in one big fight against themselves.

There is no one reason why I ended up doing some of the things that I did, and there is no one to blame but me. Three-and-a-half years ago I didn't even think there had been some wrongdoings in my life and that I was mixed up, but now I've sorted myself out a lot I can realise what a complete mess my life was, and what I was doing to myself. Maybe I am maturing.

In the sense of my physical life I was very mature by the age of 16. I enjoyed older people's company, their lifestyles and the conversations they would hold. I learned to act much older than my age, sometimes as a necessity, sometimes by choice. But I realise now that, inside, my feelings were very much those of a child.

I feel the beginning of my real life began in tragedy. That sounds very complicated at the moment, but when you read my story, I hope you will understand. That's why I want to dedicate this book to the physical victim of my early life, Trevor; and to the mental victims: my mother, brothers Adam and Simon, my sisters Rebecca and Abigail, and my father whom I didn't really know until I was 17. This is dedicated to all those very important people.

Right now I am hoping that the very words I use on these bits of paper will be the words that will eventually be typed up and printed in my book. Although I have a very basic vocabulary, I feel it is more personal for you to get in touch with me if my own words are used.

SEARCHING . . . .

Emma on the streets of Nottingham
May 28th 1988

I felt I had to leave my Nana's house. I was sick of sitting around the house, wasting my life away. There had to be something better out there for me. I had no money, and hardly any possessions worth taking. I knew that I had nowhere to go, no friends, and had never been alone in Britain before, but I was determined to get out there into the world and find something that was for me.

I did not know what lay ahead for me that night. I was nervous of what would happen. Where would I go? There was nowhere for me to go, no one to go to. I had to go out and find these things. My Nana couldn't believe what I was doing. I imagine that she felt a complete failure, and complete bewilderment. For had she not just given me a beautiful home, safe and warm, but also loved me in spite of all the things she knew I had done? I did not feel sorry for her at this time. I just wanted her to leave me alone to pack my things and go to wherever I was going.

I started throwing everything I had into my suitcase and big luggage bag. I took everything that was mine out of the bedroom: my clothes, toys, diaries, photos, 12p and the small bottle of Cognac that I had saved from my flight back to England. I felt I needed the brandy, so I opened it up and drank it, but did not feel any different. There wasn't enough to relax me or make me less apprehensive about my future.

I don't remember saying goodbye to my Nana or Aunt Pam, but I'm sure that they would have said it to me. It was dark out, as it was now about eleven in the evening. I could hardly carry my things, as they were so heavy. I felt my Nana's eyes on me as I walked out of the garden and into the crescent. A part of me wanted to turn around and go back inside and be happy with what life I had there with my relatives, but the other part of me told me to keep going, that I would find something better. I was just fighting against myself again.

With my Nana's eyes watching me leave, I stuck my head
up high into the air and walked out of the crescent as if I
didn't have a care in the world. In Canada when I ran away, I
mostly went down town if I did not have anywhere to go, so
that is where I decided to go – into Nottingham city. Surely I
would find someone who would want to take me home and
sleep with me? That I could guarantee would bring me a roof
over my head until the man had had all he wanted.

I started to walk up the rise. I could not walk fast, as I kept
stopping to put the heavy bags down. I wanted to cry,
"Please someone come along and put something new into my
life." I had seen no one on the streets. Although it was after
closing time for the pubs, this was a respectable area, and I
did not expect to see people staggering home.

A young woman was walking towards me. As she came
towards me she stopped for a minute, and looked at me. I
smiled, and went to pick up my bags and get walking again.
"Where are you going to?" she asked me. I told her casually
that I did not know where I was going. I had been at my
Nana's and got pissed off so left. She told me that I could not
just walk the streets, and that I must come to where she was
living and stay until the morning until I had decided what I
was going to do. I thought this was great. She seemed a nice
woman, and she looked clean and respectable. We walked
together back down to the bottom of the rise and went into
the house. As I walked in I did not have to look to see that it
was a dirty house, I could smell the dirtiness.

I carried on into it and was disgusted at what I saw. The
place was a dump. Everywhere was dirty, the furniture was old
and tattered, and the whole state of the place gave you the
impression that it was germ-infested. Of course I did not say
anything about this, but I think the woman, who told me her
name was Jane, was a little embarrassed about the state of
the place, and so she explained to me that it was not her house.

George owned the house. He had picked her up in a pub
one night when she had nowhere to go to, and brought her
back to stay for a while. I told her maybe I should go, that it

was not right of me to just come into someone else's house to sleep. She told me that George would not mind. "He is just a silly lonely coot, about 60 years old," she said. She told me that she did not sleep with him, and he did not pester her. I was a bit relieved to hear that, but I was still worried that it was wrong of me to walk into his house not knowing him and expect to be able to stay there for nothing.

George came down the stairs. What a tramp he looked! He was dirty and old: what you would call a dirty old man. He did not say much to Jane or myself. Jane introduced us and explained to him that I had had a row with my Nana and had nowhere to go to. George was mad at her that she had brought me back to his house. We explained my situation to him, telling him I was not on the dole, had no money, and so could not stay in a hotel. George finally was convinced and said I could stay, but I must find somewhere else to go in the morning. He didn't know I did not want to stay there myself. The place was filthy and I knew I was not really welcome, I wished I had somewhere else to go.

Jane had no job. She had a boyfriend but they were always rowing. She said she was moving out soon.

I stayed in the spare bedroom that night. It was horrible. There was just an old, dirty blood-stained bed in there and one blanket. I unpacked some of my clothes and spread them on the mattress, and used other ones to cover myself up with. All I thought of that night was the lovely clean warm bed I had left at my Nana's, but not of tomorrow. I just wanted to sleep and pretend this was not happening. I wondered if George was going to come in for sex in the night, so I left all my clothes on.

The morning came, and I didn't know what to do. I felt dirty and hungry. George and Jane told me that I must go and sign on the dole. I did not want to. I knew they did not give much money out, and the people that I had previously seen in the dole queues were people I did not want to associate myself with. "I am different, I am not one of them," I thought to myself.

I could not get over the dirtiness. I wanted a bath, but in the bathroom I was confronted with dirty clothes all over the floor, bottles of cheap toiletries with the tops off, and dust and grime everywhere. I needed a bath, so I took off my clothes and ran the water. I washed under the running water, and washed my hair. Being on my period made me feel even more dirty. I dried my hair, put clean clothes on and did my make up, but I had nowhere to go to. I told Jane and George that I was still thinking about what to do, and that I would go down to the dole office and look for somewhere to live tomorrow.

That day I just sat in the house by myself, thinking. I was hungry, but I had no money to buy any food. There wasn't any in the house, but even if there had been I would not have eaten it, because it would have been full of germs. I sat thinking about the nice flat I wanted for myself, a good job and interesting social life. I suppose I was daydreaming. That's what I did all day, thought about the things I wanted, but did nothing about getting them.

The next day came. I went through the same routine with washing – got ready, and took the bus into town, paying with the money Jane had given me. I went to the dole office, but I felt like a low-down bum doing so. I was told at the dole office that I was to go down the street to get a social security number before they could give me any money. I said I would go, but I knew inside that I could not bring myself to go to another one of these places, and so I went back to the house. I told them that I did not get any dole because I did not have a social security number, and I did not know where to go to get one. They believed me, and told me to go back to the office in the morning to ask them where I was supposed to go.

That evening, after they had been to the pub, Jane's boyfriend Mark came to the house. He was a little guy of about 25. He was as scruffy as these two, and he was a very aggressive person. George did not like Mark. Apparently Mark had caused some trouble previously. There was trouble between Mark and George, and the police were called. I tried to stay away when the police came, but I had to show my face as George was telling the police that he wanted Jane and me out of the house. I acted very calmly and explained to them that there was no problem, I was leaving in the morning, and George was a little drunk so was not really meaning what he was saying.

The police left, taking my name down as Lisa Lomax, an alias I decided on. I went to bed and started to think again. This time I thought of how I could get some money. I thought of contacting my dad, but I gave up on that thought in case he wanted me to go back to my Nana's. The only other thought was to sell my body. I knew men were attracted to me, and I was not ugly apart from only having a 29" bust. I was far from against prostitution, the only thing that held me back was wondering if I could actually go out and do it, and dare I even walk onto the street knowing that may be another girl's patch, which could cause problems and violence right away. I was frightened at the thought of going out there all by myself. I went to sleep thinking about prostitution.

The next day I told Jane what I had decided to do. She was shocked at first, but told me it was my decision. I told her it was a very easy way to make money. I suggested to her to try it with me. I tried to talk her into it, and told her I was frightened to go alone. It took a lot of trying. In the end I managed, as she said she would come with me that night. The rest of the day I spent bathing, doing my hair and thinking about the evening. I borrowed some money for Durex from Jane. All I needed now was something to wear. I cut a black skirt up and made it into a micro mini, I put on a white shirt and a silk and velvet jacket of mine, I put on tights and black stilettos. I thought it looked good, and the skirt length was something I knew people would look twice at.

Jane was very nervous about things. She made no effort to look good, and I knew she really did not want to go. We left the house at about 10.30pm and headed on up the rise to walk to the red light district. We had only got around the corner from the house when Jane decided she could not do it. No amount of persuasion would make her change her mind. I felt hurt. I did not want to go by myself, so I went back to the house with Jane. We sat talking for a while, then her boyfriend came in. We told him what I had decided to do and I dared to ask him if he would take me to work. His reply was typical, saying "Only if you paid me to do so". "No way!" was my instant thought. I am not paying this man for just coming with me to see if I could get myself a place on the street. That made me angry, and gave me the last bit of push to go out and do it. So that is what I did. A couple of minutes later I walked out of the house and headed for the beat.

It was a long walk from the house to the beat in town, but I didn't mind because I was determined to make some money for myself. As I kept on walking some of the nervousness went away, and I began to feel quite confident about what I was about to do. That was strange for me, because I had always been someone who lacked confidence in most things I did. I passed many people on their way home from the pubs, and I was very aware of the men's looks of admiration and the women's looks of envy and disgust. Halfway there and I was feeling pretty good in myself.

A taxi passed me going in the opposite direction, and I caught the eyes of the driver looking at me. He drove past and I thought nothing of him, when a couple of minutes later the same taxi drove up beside me going in my direction. He opened the door and asked me where I was heading, and I told him Forest Road (the beat). He offered to drive me there, so I got in. His name was Pete. He wasn't particularly good-looking, but he was not ugly either. He seemed OK. I laughed when he told me he thought I was going up Forest Road. Did I look like I was walking up the street to sell my body? I didn't think so.

I didn't really know the whereabouts on the beat; I wanted to be dropped off, so we drove around for a little while. I told him I had never worked in this way in England before, and he turned out to be pretty helpful, telling me places I could take my clients in the car for business, and where the best place to stand was. He also told me that the common price on Motts Street was £10. I thought this a very low price compared to the prices charged in Canada.

He drove into Forest Road and parked. I guess he figured he had a good thing here – a nice-looking, vulnerable young girl in his car. We chatted in the car for a while and then he started to come on to me. I did not resist. Why, the guy had done me a favour, and it was obvious he knew the Vice score pretty well, and I did not want to start my first night on a bad note, so we had sex in the car and then he dropped me off at an empty corner. He gave me his name and car number, and told me to ring for him any time if I was in trouble. Also, he said his firm was very reliable.

There I was, my place of work. It was very strange that, when I started to pace up the street, it felt like I had been doing it for years. I felt at home. It was such a strange feeling, like that is where I belonged. Well, had I not done it many times? Sold my body for something I wanted? Are not all women on parade to men's lustful eyes? Yes, they are. The only difference for me at that moment was that I was going to start to get something out of men's sexual needs and desires.

My first client came along. He looked clean and his car was clean, so I felt even better and I got in. He did not talk much, but he was very keen on getting a blow job. I did not like the thought of this, so I kept telling him "no way". He was very persuasive, so in the end I agreed he could have a blowjob with a Durex, and with all my clothes on, for £15. I took time in all my actions so as to keep my face away from his body for as long as possible. As soon as my lips were around his penis it was a very short time until he came. A couple of minutes and it was over, and I had £15 in my purse. I felt better than ever, and I knew then that from now on that I was never going to let men just have me for nothing. I had something they wanted, and they had something that I wanted, so it was going to be fair exchanges.

I went home after that one client. It was late, and I had

enough money to survive on until the next night. I went back to the house with a great sense of accomplishment. I had been and done something that I had been doing for ages, yet this time I had got something out of it for myself that I needed. The next morning I was able to buy something to eat. I didn't want a big meal or anything, so I just got myself a doughnut and a block of cheese from the corner shop. It felt good to eat something. The rest of the day I spent looking for somewhere to live. I looked in the paper for flats close to the beat, but there weren't many. I found one and phoned to make arrangements to see it, but when I got there I was told it was already taken. I felt great disappointment, and just didn't know what to do or where to go. I went back to the house and found a hotel, where I booked a room for the night. I went there and dropped my things off and then went straight back out to work.

That evening I positioned myself on a nice bus corner where there was a constant flow of traffic and pedestrians. I also saw quite a few of the other girls out and about in that area. None of them made any attempt to make conversation, but I did get a few smiles from some. After I had my first client I came back to the same spot. There were a lot of girls here when I returned, but I stood at my same spot and just kept working.

I was standing next to the phone box when a man in a red car drove past and stopped in a driveway across the street. It was very obvious that he wanted business, but there were so many girls between him and me that I did not even bother to walk towards the car. A bleached-blonde girl about the same age as me approached. After a few minutes of conversation, she closed the door again and started to walk towards me. After a couple of steps she looked up at me, and with a very unfriendly voice said: "He wants you." I was pleased, of course, but I wondered if I was being a bit cheeky going on to the streets not knowing whose patch it was, and taking over their might-have-been business. "To hell with it," I thought, "every woman is for herself in this game."

Meeting Trevor Armitage

I walked over and got in. He was another clean-looking punter with a nice car, so things seemed OK. He was quite a friendly guy and we got chatting straight away. He wanted straight sex, but he did not want to go to my regular spot for it so we drove away behind the beat and into a school courtyard. He asked me a bit about myself. I told him that I was 16, and just back from Canada this year, and that I did not have anywhere to live. He offered me a place to stay immediately. I did not think it was strange for him to do so. What man would turn down a woman to stay with him if she is young, good-looking and obviously gives out sex like it's nothing?

He explained that he had his own house, two cars, a job in the daytime in Leicester, and a job helping out in the pub his parents owned. So far things sounded pretty good. Obviously he had his own money, so he did not want me to stay with him so he could take my money. He was not my idea of a good-looking guy, as he looked middle-aged, thick-skinned, and smartly dressed in a suit and tie. One thing that was very noticeable was his big smile with perfect teeth; he also smiled with his eyes so I decided that was the best thing about him.

I was very curious as to why someone with what he had would want to offer a prostitute he had just met a place to stay. He explained to me that he was living with this woman, but the relationship was over and the woman was taking her time to get out of the house. As soon as she moved out I could move in, he said. That sounded strange. I wondered if she was another prostitute that he wanted out of his house. He gave me his phone number and arranged that I would phone him after I had finished work the next night. He asked me if I wanted to be driven back to work but I didn't, so I asked him to drive me back to the hotel where I was staying for the night. I paid my room bill and went up to sleep. I wondered what would ever come out of my client's offer, and went to sleep thinking I probably would never see him again.

I did not like the hotel I was staying in, as it was too far away from my place of work and would cost me a fortune in taxi fares, so I packed up and went back to the house. Of course Jane and George were not too pleased to see me, but they let me come in. I went shopping that day and got myself some new make up, some clothes and lots of Durex. In the evening I went out to work, took a couple of clients and then phoned yesterday's client, whose name was Trevor. He was surprised that I was finished work so early, but said he would pick me up straightaway. He explained that he was waiting for his parents to close up the pub, before we would go back there and open it up again. We passed the time driving around talking. I told him more about myself, and he seemed very interested.

As the time went on to 11p.m. we drove to the pub and opened it up for ourselves. It was a cute place, which had a warm feeling to it. There were two rooms to it, one that he called the noisy room and the other he called the quiet room. We went into the noisy room, put on the jukebox and sat drinking for ages. My alcohol resistance was very low at this time, as I had not had a drink for quite a while, so I was getting quite tipsy. He told me there was a room above the pub where I could stay until the woman in his house left. We drank some more and listened to music, then had sex on the seats in the pub. Later we went upstairs where I went straight to sleep until the morning, when I woke up at 5.30am.

Before calling a taxi to go back to the house, we arranged that when I left the house that evening to go to work I would bring all my things and leave them at the pub, where I would stay from now on. Things did not work out according to plan. I left for work in a taxi with all my things, but when I went to the pub Trevor told me that I was too early, that his parents were still there and he didn't want them knowing I would be staying. So I transferred all my things from the taxi into Trevor's car and took the taxi up to the beat to work. I worked until 11p.m. when Trevor came and picked me up to go back to the pub as arranged.

When we got there we had a couple of drinks, then decided that he would take me back to his house so the woman could see Trevor was serious that he wanted her to move out. Also, he wanted me to see the house before I decided to move in with him. I did not know what I was walking into, and I didn't know what the woman's reactions would be towards me, so I decided I would play Miss Cool. I walked into the house like I had been there many times before.

The house was comfortable, semi-detached and clean. It was simply furnished, so spacious looking. The living room was beige and dark brown, with an open gas fire and a huge window that looked out over the back garden. It had three bedrooms. The front bedroom was to be Trevor's and mine, and the two back bedrooms were not furnished but contained luggage, bags, photography equipment, and other junk. There was a bathroom upstairs and toilet downstairs, across from the small kitchen. It was clean, warm, and comfortable, and I knew I would like it.

I kicked off my shoes and curled up comfortably in the chair. I was amazed at how different the woman was to me. She was middle-aged, quite respectable and quiet looking, yet she did have a worn, hard look to her face. I was not at all polite to her, and started to ask her personal questions as to why she had not moved out of the house yet as Trevor wanted her out. She told me that she had not yet found anywhere to live and that this was just as much her place as his, as she insisted that she was paying the mortgage on the place too. I didn't know whether to believe her, so I was just neutral and explained to her that I did not care where she went to sleep that night, but I was sleeping in his bed with him so she had to find somewhere else.

I was impressed with the house. It was in a nice area, and I liked it right away. We left the house and he took me to a club called The Bables that was right next door to his parents' pub. We did not have to pay to get in, as he knew the owners pretty well. This was a club that I had been into as a child, with my mother. I did not remember the actual layout of it, but I could remember the lights from my childhood, and I could remember that my mother was always talking of the place when I was a child. It wasn't very big.

That night we went back to Trevor's again, and she was still there. I wondered why she had not moved out of the house when he wanted her out? Why was she still there? She told me she was looking for somewhere to live, and that it was half her house because she was paying half the mortgage. It didn't matter what answer she could give me, all I knew is me and Trevor wanted her out.

Why she didn't hit me, I don't know. I was very rude when I explained to her I didn't care where she slept that night, but she wasn't sleeping in Trevor's bed because that's where I was sleeping. She didn't say anything, but I could tell she was annoyed. Apparently she had been sleeping at the house, and Trevor sleeping at his parents' pub. I put my shoes back on and Trevor and I left.

Trevor and I went to The Bables Club again. I had begun to acquire a taste for sweet Martini, which was quite nice to have a couple of drinks of in the evening. It also made life feel better. I danced with a lot of different men, and had a good time. I liked to look good for myself to feel good, and when I looked good I knew other people thought I looked good. I turned many heads in my micro mini, and I beamed with confidence. Trevor seemed very proud of me – introducing me to everyone, smiling all the time.

We opened up the pub again. I tried my hand at a game of pool – something I thought myself pretty good at, but Trevor completely blew me out. Me being a bit tipsy didn't help either. Trevor danced by himself while I sat drinking. As soon as he started to dance I saw something feminine about him. He danced softly, and seemed deep in thought. His dancing didn't suit the way I thought of him. In my mind, I then vowed I'd never dance with him.

I was quite looking forward to another confrontation with Elizabeth back at the house. But when we returned she was asleep on the couch. Being a bitch, I made as much noise as possible, and then Trevor and I went to bed.

In the morning Elizabeth was still in the house. Before she left to go to work, she pulled out some official papers to try to prove to me she owned half the house. I wasn't interested and she gathered that. I just explained I didn't care what the situation was; all I wanted was to move in and live with Trevor. Soon after, she left the house to go to work.

Trevor bathed, then I went into the bath. I filled it with lots of bubbles, tied my hair back and put on a face-mask. It felt good to be in clean surroundings again. I'd closed the door as I am not one to flaunt my body (due to not liking certain parts of it), and I didn't want Trevor to see the face-mask. I didn't expect him to walk in, but he did. I almost died of embarrassment as he stood in the doorway, laughing uncontrollably. Strong words told him to get out so he left, still chuckling at the state of me. I put on his bathrobe, and while he went to the chip shop for our dinner, I sat and applied my make-up and blow-dried my hair. We sat in the living room. Trevor kept staring at me, which made me feel uncomfortable for a while, but then I started to giggle a lot, remembering my earlier embarrassment in the bathroom.

I know I was living in his nice house paying no bills, buying no food, and never paying when we were out, but he was getting sex free any time he wanted it, so I felt I should keep my own money as I owed him nothing. I didn't think he was stealing it, or expected my money, but it had just got to be a habit to give it to him, a habit I felt had to stop. So I started not giving it to him. I would still drop in at the pub between clients, but only for a drink, and I would leave again soon after with the same amount of money. There are not many places to hide money on yourself when you could be asked to do a full strip at any time, so I decided the best place for it was somewhere in the small handbags I would carry. I went out and bought myself a purse-size panty liner case, and would pack about four panty liners in. After each client I would fold the bills up nearly and squash them in between the liners.

Trevor never asked for money, but I knew he was a bit

upset I wasn't giving him any of it any more. He didn't say anything directly, but sometimes he would make remarks as to where the money was going. He would ask, was I saving up to go back to Canada to leave him, was I saving up to get a place of my own? I could not answer yes to any of these questions. I wasn't saving up, I just wanted money of my own to spend when I wanted, and how I wanted.

I think he was going through a state of being paranoid that I was going to leave him. Because I had not unpacked my suitcase, he made comments as to whether or not I was just staying with him until someone or something else came along. That was not the case either. I was never short of offers for a place to stay from men who wanted sex, but I never left. I didn't want that. Knowing that Trevor worried maybe one day he would come home and find me gone made me feel that maybe he did care about me and want me there, not just for sex, but because he also liked me as a person. This made me feel better inside, more willing to relax and unpack my things, and really live there.

The day I unpacked, he noticed straight away. He was really pleased, I could tell. I told him 'sorry' but that I had decided to stay, and he would have to put up with me for a long time. Our relationship started to grow from then on. I started looking at the house as my home, and Trevor as my man. I still did not love him, but I was beginning to really like him.

His feelings for me became more apparent as time went on. Some days he would phone me from work five times or more a day to tell me he loved me, but maybe he was just checking to see if I was at home. He started to show more affection outside of bed. Sometimes on a weekend, after he had been working at his parent's pub, he would come home with flowers for me. He started to take care that I ate every day by buying the things I liked. Sometimes we would have a bag of chips, but not often. He always made sure I had plenty of Durex and lots of stockings and tights for work. We began living as girlfriend and boyfriend. He drove me to work every night, or I would take a taxi if I was not leaving until after he wanted to go to work at the pub. He would always pick me up on my corner at 11p.m. or I would get a taxi to the pub, as eleven was the time he wanted me off the streets. I didn't stay out later than that if I could help it.

I had only been working after 11.p.m. once or twice before this particular occasion. I had my last client at about 11.15 one night. I knew I was late, but I didn't think Trevor would mind. He was an oldish man whom I had never seen before. He wanted straight sex, so we went behind the school and parked the car. The guy wanted me stripped, so after arranging the price I took off my clothes. I put the Durex on, masturbating him for a while, and then he jumped on top of me for intercourse. No sooner had he got on me than both the front car doors opened and a flashlight shone in. It was the Vice squad. I wasn't frightened, I was pissed off I had been caught. I'd heard rumours that they did not charge you the first few times, so I wasn't worried about being in a cell all night.

My client got into his own seat and pulled his trousers back on. I put on my top, then got out of the car to straighten my skirt up and put on my shoes. One of the Vice squad took me to the vehicle they were using, which was a Land Rover, and the other guy stayed to talk to my client. My arresting officer was OK, and chatty enough. They told me they would have to take me down to the station to caution me about prostitution. That was fine by me, as I knew I would be home the same night. They asked me all sorts of questions as to why I did it, did I have a ponce, and wanted the usual details as to where I was living, how old I was, etc. My handbag was searched and all its contents listed. I was warned of the dangers of prostitution, but of course I wasn't listening. I received my first caution.

I was fingerprinted and photographed, then they wanted to drive me home to see what conditions I was living in and whom I was living with. I knew they would suspect Trevor of poncing me, forcing me onto the streets, so I pretended that he didn't know I was a prostitute and asked if they would tell him that I had been picked up for something else. When we

got to the house Trevor was in bed sleeping, but he got up
when he heard the vehicle outside of the house. When he
looked out of the bedroom window he must wondered what
I was doing, bringing two men back to the house. He was
wary at first, but when he realised it was the Vice squad I
could tell by his face that he was pretty pissed off with me.

The officer who stayed with me most of the time, Sergeant
Mike, took me into the living room and the other one took
Trevor into the kitchen to talk. I poured myself a drink of
Martini immediately. Mike told me that 'of course' Trevor knew
I was a whore, and asked me again if he was my ponce. After
a few minutes they came out of the kitchen and soon left.

Trevor was not happy, and lectured me about what he had
said in the past about being off the streets by 11p.m. He told
me I was stupid, which didn't make me feel better about
being picked up. Trevor then told me the Vice squad advised
him to get rid of me, because I was trouble. I thought that
was funny, so I asked him if he was taking their advice. "Of
course not," he said. He went back to bed and I followed
him soon after. Trevor later confessed that he thought I had
run off for the night when I was so late coming home.

I started to drink more during the days, because it made
me feel better and more relaxed. I started to have a Martini
and vitamins for my breakfast, and to get obsessed with
cleanliness. I would clean the house from top to bottom with
bottles of bleach and disinfectant. I did several loads of
washing every day, and used disinfectant in the wash water. I
bathed myself about three times a day using lots of Dettol in
the water.

Sometimes I would go out shopping. I hated trying to find
clothes that fitted me as everything needed altering, so for
the winter I decided to buy a couple of long coats to cover
me, and just buy shirts and nice jumpers to wear with a belt
and stockings. I enjoyed buying shoes and handbags to match.
My favorite shop was Boots. Every time I went in I would
spend £50-£80 on cosmetics, Dettol, health drinks and
vitamins. That was my last port of call on a shopping day, and

I would not leave the shop until I only had enough money for a taxi home. Sometimes that meant buying makeup that I would never use because I didn't like the colour. I enjoyed spending money.

I worked every night, never missing one, and I worked hard. I believe Trevor often helped himself to my money, as I never counted it so never knew exactly how much I had. But sometimes I would come down in the morning and I wouldn't even have a penny in my bag. That would get me cross. But he insisted that he only borrowed it because he needed it. Only once did I ever see it returned, and that was one time when he had helped himself to a large amount, and I demanded it back. It didn't really bother me too much him having my money, but if he had asked instead of just taking it I would have been happier about it. I didn't believe he needed it either. He worked all day and most nights, so why did he need my wages as well?

I had begun to get friendly with most of the taxi drivers down at DG Taxis, as I used them at least once a day, sometimes five times. They were very good to me. I always got a driver straight away and they were always polite. I often saw Pete driving around the beat, and he regularly stopped to chat.

After I had been living with Trevor for a while, he started to become jealous of other men. Sometimes when we were at Bables I would go off dancing with other men for a long time. I went to Trevor in between dances, but I would never dance with him. People liked me there. I wasn't too much of a flirt, although I knew people found me attractive, so I did play on that. The bouncers at the door used to tease Trevor about buying me a skirt or dress that fitted, as my skirts were always so short, but I liked to show off my legs.

Occasionally I would go back to the bar and Trevor would be gone. The first time that happened I got worried, I counted on him always being at my side. I couldn't find him anywhere, so I went next door to see if he had opened up the pub and found him there. He was just sat by himself, drinking and listening to music. I was cross that he had left me alone there, and for not telling me he was leaving. He was pretty pissed off, and told me that it was obvious I was having fun without him, so he decided to leave me to it. He was sarcastic in the way he said it. We stayed in the pub for a couple more drinks, then went home.

Trevor left me in the club on my own a few times after that. I got in a habit of finding out where he was, so I didn't need to rush around straightaway. One time when he left me, I stayed dancing and drinking until closing time. When I went next door to find him he wasn't there, so I was really pissed off. He left me stranded at a club with no money. (I never took money out with me, as I never expected to pay for anything.) I phoned home and there he was. Boy, I was mad. I let him know how cross I was about it, but he still wouldn't come and pick me up. He told me to take a taxi home and he would have the money ready his end.

Trevor was in a mood when I got home, sitting there drinking a lager. He started saying I would rather be out with other men than with him, and that I didn't want him around when I was having fun anyway. I wasn't in the mood for arguing so I sat there drinking, listening to the music, ignoring him. He went up to bed soon after and I fell asleep on the couch. I woke up in the early morning and went to bed.

I started to phone my mum regularly. We would gossip and I would talk to Adam and Simon a lot. Also Abigail was at home sometimes, so I would talk to her too. I tried to get my mum to talk about her life and how she was doing, but she was always very distant when it came to talking about herself. Deep down I knew she was still unhappy.

Mum had a new boyfriend called Alex. He was a lot younger than her, but she insisted he was a decent guy, he had a job and he liked Adam and Simon, something that was very important to me. Apart from my mom, Adam and Simon were still my number one people. I would talk to Alex sometimes, and he seemed OK from a distance, but then didn't everyone? I used to have a laugh with him, and sometimes we would talk dirty, but nothing serious. When I was drunk, and Mom and Alex were drunk, sometimes we would stay on the phone for over an hour gossiping and joking around. I never worried about the phone bill at the end of it all. I never seemed to worry about tomorrow, I just concentrated on getting through every today.

Sometimes Susan, my friend from the children's home in Canada, and I would talk. We mostly talked about our past together, and what we would do if we were together again. We still cared about each other very much, and were still as close as two sisters. Trevor got the wrong impression about our relationship, and soon became jealous of Susan. He thought I was going to save my money and go back to Canada to be with Susan. Sometimes that actually felt like a great idea, but other times I was happy and content with my life with Trevor. I had a couple of calls with Jose, my other friend from Canada, but after a while Sue and Jose became lost in my mind and I only phoned my mother.

I phoned my Nana to say that I was well and living with a man who had a nice house in a nice area. She told me there was some mail at the house, so I arranged to go and pick it up at the end of the week. Trevor stopped at my Nana's house for me one evening. He wanted to come in and meet her but I didn't want him to, so he stayed out in the car. There was a funny atmosphere between my Nan and I. I could tell she was still hurt from me leaving her. I did not stop for more than a couple of minutes, but I asked how they all were and that was it. The mail she gave me was from The Mary Poplins Nanny Agency, telling me they had accepted me to go on a two-year training course. I didn't think much about this, but I did wonder if my life would have been better if I had stuck around and gone on the training course.

Trevor was very close and warm towards me, yet he was so far away at times. All he ever talked about was our life, and my life, he never discussed himself. I learnt he had a son, the young boy I would see working behind the bar in the pub some nights. He was quite good looking, tall, blond, with a beautiful big smile like his dad. Steven was 15, just some months younger than me, and lived with his mother. Trevor never talked about Steven's mother and I never asked, but I knew they only lived a little way away.

The first time I actually met Steven was one Sunday lunchtime soon after I moved in. Trevor was out working in the pub as usual until lunchtime. When he came home he brought Steven back with him. I was quite annoyed at first: I was only wearing Trevor's bathrobe, and I had on a mud mask, so I looked a right state. Trevor thought it was quite funny. I ignored the laughter from him and sat on the couch giving myself a manicure. Steven wanted some money from his dad. Trevor pulled out a big wad of money, and gave him just a small amount. Steven wasn't happy and wanted more, which Trevor gave him. Steven left soon after. He looked a good kid, a bit arrogant, but then again a nice-looking boy like that has every right to be.

I started to have feelings of love for Trevor. I can't pinpoint why I loved him, it was just that I found my life with him nice and comforting. He was definitely beginning to show deep feelings for me. Trevor had the patience of a saint with me. Sometimes I was very awkward to live with, as I often would get very depressed and be a total misery, sitting drinking and crying for hours. Often I cried because I wanted to go home to Canada. Life seemed so much better over there now I had left. I wanted to be with my mum, I wanted to feel the glamorous life in Canada.

The Violence

In his love ,Trevor became very jealous and possessive over me. Some of his jealousy was comforting, giving me more reason to think he loved me. But when the jealousy started to turn to violence, it was a different story. The first time he hit me was over something very trivial, but it stemmed from his jealousy. I had been late home one night, only by about fifteen minutes, but that was enough to put him in a bad

mood. I sat as usual having a drink when I came in, and
Trevor was there with his. He didn't look too pissed off, but
he was very sulky.

I was telling him how my evening was, any unusual clients,
any trouble etc., when I happened to mention that I had seen
Pete, and that he had offered me a place to stay if I wanted it.
Pete had told me he would keep a lookout for anything, and
that he now had his own place. I didn't have a chance to
explain to Trevor that I was happy with him, and didn't want
to go to live with anyone else, before he lost his temper. He
grabbed me by the hair and started hitting me around the
head. He was screaming at me that I was a dirty slag, and
screaming Pete's name at me. I was frightened of him, as his
temper really seemed to have gone.

Trevor dragged me out into the hallway and started hitting
my head against the wall. That hurt like hell. All I did was
keep my face covered, as that was the most precious thing to
me. He opened the front door with one hand ready to throw
me out, but then changed his mind and closed it again.
Trevor let go of me at that stage and went to bed. I moved
into the living room and sat there crying, because I was so
hurt by what he had done. I knew that any bruises would
heal, but it was the mental pain from the incident that hurt
me more. While he was hitting me I told him over and over
again that I was happy with him and I did not want to leave.

Maybe he did believe me in the end, as he let me go. I was
sad and annoyed at what he had done to me. One part of me
wanted to rush upstairs for a cuddle from him because I felt
rotten inside, another part of me wanted to never speak to
him again, and to treat him like he deserved to be treated for
what he just did. I stayed downstairs for a while, then I went
up to bed. I was still upset, but I needed to be next to him
and feel loved. I was still crying a bit, and Trevor comforted
me with cuddles and affection. Soon after I went to sleep.

I was angrier with him in the morning. I found it very hard
to look at him or talk to him. I felt very uneasy. He said he
was sorry, that he was just frightened of losing me, and I

believed him. I still felt he was wrong and kept away from him for a couple of days after, but soon it was almost forgotten. I started to have mixed-up feelings for him, and felt split in two. I knew I loved him, but 'how' and 'why' were beginning to get mixed up.

There were two parts of me. The prostitute me, who was strong, never needed anyone, confident and very professional. Then there was the young girl me, who wanted lots of love and attention. I wanted to be pampered, and cared for. This me wanted to settle down into a normal relationship situation. This me wanted Trevor to love me like a father. Trevor saw the different me's a lot. When I started to get mixed up he could notice that the two me's were clashing together, that I was not keeping them separate anymore. He once commented to me that he didn't know who I was at any one time anymore. Was I Lisa the prostitute, or Emma the girl whom he didn't see much of in the beginning?

I liked the affection he gave me, but the sex became a problem. The two me's came into our physical relationship also. I responded to all his affection outside of bed, and enjoyed it. In bed I responded to heavy petting, and oral sex, but as soon as intercourse came into it I turned back into the prostitute I was. All my feelings of warmth and comfort would turn cold. I hated intercourse: it was like a feeling of violation. It became something I dreaded. No matter how much I enjoyed petting, I knew in the end he would want intercourse. Sex for Trevor was every night, sometimes more than once. When I turned cold I don't think he knew the difference, as I continued to do everything to make out I was enjoying it. We never talked about it, and things just continued the same as they were. Trevor didn't have any unusual kinks and he was always affectionate, so I thought it was not really his fault.

Since the first time he hit me, things started to get worse in our relationship. I wanted him to love me as a best friend, not as a jealous boyfriend. He started to drive around the

beat more often at nighttime, he started to go through my
handbag and personal things, and he wanted to know what I
did all evening out working. Sometimes he would like me to
tell him what I had done for my clients, and what were they
like. If he was in a bad mood he would insist that I enjoyed
my clients, and call me a slag. p. 125

I know he wanted me to give up my work as a prostitute,
but he didn't understand that I wanted to continue to work
to keep my independence. He often spoke of wishing he had
met me in a different way, rather than being my client. I think
he only wanted that so he could condemn my work, and
would really lecture me about it in a bid to make me stop.

My work was like a different life. It brought me money,
which was the main thing. I knew the beat and the set-up of
things pretty well now. I gave up using my alias Lisa and
started to use my proper name. The Vice squad knew me
now, so there was no one I needed to hide from. I liked the
name Butterfly for a street name, so that is what I used
sometimes. I guess I picked it up from flying from one section
of the beat to another on bad business nights, in a bid to find
clients.

I started to get friendly with another young girl who had
started to work. Her name was Viki, and she had a ponce. I
hated the thought of her working her backside off all night
just to give some guy money for draw and gold. Her ponce
was her sister's ex-ponce, which doesn't say much. I talked of
my feelings to her. I tried to get her to think differently
towards him, but she was only a child inside and she was
convinced the guy loved her. He beat her and she was not
very well dressed for a whore, but she was content and
secure like me, and so she was staying with him. We often
exchanged clients if it was all right with them. I would not go
to houses or take a client to my house and she would not do
oral sex, so working the same corner we made a good team.

Trevor took me to a pub that was only a minute's walk
down my street. It was called Fosters. It was a small, cosy
place, and clean. The owner was friends with Trevor, so I

quickly got introduced and became a regular in there. Trevor took me there occasionally, but after a while I started to go in a lot by myself between clients. I liked it in there. The owner, Hans was always friendly to me and seemed a good laugh to be with. I started to drink vodka. I had got to the point of drinking a big bottle of Martini in the day, but it was not doing anything for me. So I started to drink vodka and lemonade or vodka and Babycham. I didn't like the taste of vodka, so I never drank it straight.

The Indian man in the corner shop was a good guy, and was married with two kids. Him and his father ran the shop, and often he would have his children in there. He was good to us working girls though. He always stocked lots of Durex, and if the Vice squad were patrolling the beat a lot he would let us hide out in his shop for a while. He was polite and always asking where I had been if I hadn't been in for a couple of days.

Me and the other girls made no effort to talk to each other. I only saw them on my beat when they wanted the shop, apart from that they stayed away, which I appreciated. We said "hello" in passing, and gave each other information on the Vice squad when we had some. There were a lot of real hags out there on the streets. They looked such messes. Scruffy clothes, no make up, hair like rats' tails, real scruffs to look at. They may have been nice girls, but they had lost their self-respect somewhere along the way. That was something I hoped I would never lose.

It frightened me to see these girls sometimes. It was the thought that maybe in a few years I would end up like that. I didn't want that. Another thing I noticed is that none of the scruffs that were working down the other end came up to the shop at all. I'd only see them at a distance while driving somewhere. Maybe they didn't use Durex, so didn't need to use the shop? Often Victoria would come out to work for the night with no money to buy Durex. That wasn't her fault, as her ponce took all her money, so I always made sure I took a lot out with me so I would have enough to get her a few. I felt sorry for her. She was a young pretty girl who could make a better life than that.

There was another girl I felt sorry for. She was a right mixed-up person, and an absolute scruff. She had a sloppy body, tatty clothes, bleached blonde hair and never wore any make up. I never saw her take any clients either. She was about 22, but very immature. There was a time when she would come out to work with stories about having babies. One day she was pregnant, the next day she had had a miscarriage, the next day she had had an abortion. I wondered what her hang-up on pregnancy was, and that maybe she was like me and longed to be pregnant.

One night she was in a real state. She didn't have anywhere to stay, and she had no money. I invited her to stay with me, and at first she said she'd like to. I took her back to the house and gave her some old makeup to put on, and a dress that was too big for me, along with one of my long coats to wear, and a handbag to match her shoes. She looked much better, but there was still room for improvement. She curled her hair, we had a drink, and I phoned Trevor to see if it would be all right if she stayed over, which it was.

We took a taxi back out to work that night. Some bum in a cheap car came along and picked her up. We arranged to meet up at a certain time to go back to the house after work. But somehow I knew I wouldn't see her again that night. I didn't, and I didn't see her again for a long time. When she turned up again, she told me she had been in hospital after a bad miscarriage. I knew not to believe her stories, but I played her game and showed concern for her well-being. Inside I realised that there was no point in me trying to help the girl if she didn't want to help herself, so I gave up giving her the attention she was after.

I had built up quite a few regulars after a while. Most of them wanted intercourse or oral sex, but a few were different demands. I never had any problems with my regulars; I suppose I became a friend to some of them. They would tell me about their lives, and I would always be honest and friendly to them. My most regular guy was one called Mike. He was a clean, tall, dark man, and spoke very softly for the type of guy he looked. I guess I always expected him to speak in a real dark voice. I enjoyed seeing this Mike. He let me get some of my anger out on him.

Of course, I didn't get any physical pleasure, but the mental pleasure of forcing his trousers off and handling him roughly allowed me to be a bit vicious. That's what he liked me to do. He wanted me to act the wild horny woman. He wanted to be the wife-faithful shy guy. He would fight with me not to get into his trousers, but we both knew what the limits were. He never really took much work, as he always had a hard-on as soon as I got into the car. I saw him at least once a week, sometimes more.

At one point he was desperate for me to go home with him for business, so we could do it in front of his wife. He begged and begged me. He told me his wife knew about us, that he would pay me good, and that there would never be any trouble. He wanted me to bring off his wife after I had finished with him. I felt sorry for him, but it was something I would not do. I would not go to a house where I didn't know who was going to be inside apart from his wife. The thought of things getting touchy while I was trapped in a house with two people didn't appeal to me. He was terribly upset that I wouldn't go with him.

I had a lot of punters. Some of them would come back, others I think were one-time try-outs. My favourite guy was an Italian pilot. I had never had such a clean, immaculate punter in all my life. He was fairly good-looking for his age. To me he would have made a perfect sugar daddy. I didn't say that to him, but one time he told me he had just recently married an 18-year-old Italian girl. He was in his early forties. I wondered if he had met her as a prostitute. He seemed to love her in his own way, as after I knew she existed he often spoke of her. This guy seemed so perfect in every way. I didn't see him too often, but often enough to get a nice surprise seeing him waiting on the corner for me. He brought me chocolates a couple of times, nice individually wrapped ones. I either took them home with me straight away or I carried them around all night. I think I only saw him on his flights that he had to stay over on. He always treated me well.

I met Toni just after things started to go wrong between Trevor and me. Toni waited while I took one punter for business and came back. He told me he only wanted to talk, so I promised that I would take him for my last client, even though it would be after 11p.m., the time Trevor wanted me beside him wherever he was. I wasn't too worried, though. I knew I wouldn't be over an hour late, and there is no way I was going to turn down getting money for just talking to someone.

I took my last punter and jumped into Toni's car. He was more a rugged kind of guy. He wasn't bad looking, and he was polite and OK to me. He was also clean. The first time I met him he paid me straightaway, and we went and parked outside the police station and talked. I can't really remember what we talked about, but I know 99% of it was about me. He wanted to know all about me. He told me he had been waiting around watching me for quite a while. He wanted to catch me at a time when I was not too busy, which wasn't too often. I remember asking him why he wanted to talk to me, and all he said was he was interested, that's all.

He had no sexual intentions; he never got a hard-on at all through this session with him. He was OK. It was getting late, and I could see he wanted to sit there for much longer listening to me tell him about myself. I told him that I had to be at home over half-an-hour ago, so he offered to drive me. I knew things at home were going to be off, and I was right. All my stuff was packed up and on the doorstep waiting for me. I was right angry. I wasn't even an hour late, and was not prepared to start arguing, so I thought: "Fine, you just throw me out, and see if I come crawling back."

I was vexed that I had dropped off most of my night's earnings at the house earlier on in the evening, so I only had a bit of money on me. I wanted to start an argument about that, but Toni advised me not to. He put my stuff in his car and we drove down the road and sat and talked for a while. I guess in that next half-hour I told him quite a bit about myself and my relationship with Trevor. His advice was to leave him for good, and start up on my own. I didn't know what the hell I wanted to do, but at that very moment I just wanted to sit down somewhere and have a drink.

Toni checked us into the Savoy hotel. This guy was very distant as far as his life went, and I never did find out much about him. His idea was that I should stay the night in the hotel, then go down the social in the morning, quit prostitution, get a house and a proper job. God, that didn't appeal to me. I didn't feel strong enough even to consider going on with life alone without someone looking out for me. I was in a mess. He got us some drinks up to the room, so I felt OK for a while. I knew I couldn't sleep that night, not knowing what tomorrow was going to be like. We talked a lot. He told me he was married to a good wife, that he worked in the chip shop business, and that was all I really found out about him. We had sex. He didn't pay for it, and I didn't ask for any money as I felt I owed it to him for his trouble and for paying for the hotel room.

After sex we had a bath, then he wanted to leave. There's nothing worse for me than having to sleep alone. It's not the sex I need, but the closeness and comfort. It was now five hours later and I was pretty sure Trevor would have clamed down by now, and I was 100% sure he regretted what he had done and wanted me to come back, so I decided to give him a call. "Yes, I could go straight home," he said, and "No", he promised there would be no fighting. I believed him. He sounded all sad and sorry on the phone, so I got Toni to drive me home.

Things were fine when I got home, because Trevor did not want to fight. I told him why I had been late, and that I could not turn down money for talking to a client. He explained to me that he had thrown me out because he was sure I had found someone better than him and had run off. Incidents like this often brought us closer. Even if we fought and I got a pasting from him, I was sure to find out more about how much he cared for me. I guess incidents like this were the times when we had the most communication between us. We went to bed as happy as could be that night. I never thought I would see Toni again.

I was to see more of Toni. I would see him driving around the beat occasionally. He would stop for a chat, and ask me how I was doing. If I was busy he'd soon go, but if it was a quiet evening, or I felt like taking a break, we'd go pick up a bottle, and go out of town somewhere, and sit talking. That's all we ever did. He did the listening, and I did the talking. It was a break, something different, and I thought he was OK. He either dropped me back off at work, or somewhere where I'd planned to meet Trevor.

Trevor picked me up at work one night soon after this incident and we went into town to drink. We met up with one of his friends who took an instant dislike to me. I think he knew of my occupation and was prejudiced against prostitutes. We had quite a good slanging match between us. I never minded things like that. I always got through slaggings by looking down on the other person. I'd gotten pretty good at walking with my head up in the clouds, and looking down on other people as if they were scum of the earth.

I guess sometimes I came across as being a bit of a snob and uninterested in people around me. I didn't like to mix too much. I think I built a wall up around me for some kind of protection against being rejected or something. Although I liked the company of everyday working-class people, I always thought myself better than them, and always believed that I was meant for a life of glamour, wealth, security, and lots of love. (Maybe it has always been a dream, but I feel I will one day be above the normal everyday person.)

When it was closing time me, Trevor and his friend went off and opened up his parents' pub and sat in there for a while drinking. The insults between his friend and me were still flying, and I think that Trevor felt mighty uncomfortable, so soon as we got there we left. The friend went next door to Bables and we headed home. We took the route home that took us along the beat and past my corner. When we drove past we saw Toni waiting there for me. Toni saw us, but I didn't acknowledge his presence. Trevor made some remark, which I refused to answer, I thought it was best to ignore it all. So we just carried on home.

Once at home, Trevor went straight to bed. I put on the music, poured a drink and phoned my mother to see what was up with her that day. I was getting right into the conversation with her when I heard a knock at the door. At first I thought it might be Trevor's friend so I was going to ignore it, but curiosity got the better of me and I went to see who it was. I couldn't open the door because Trevor had locked it and taken the keys up to bed with him, so I looked out of the kitchen window and saw Toni standing there. I was glad to see him because I liked him, but I knew this was going to create problems. Trevor hated him. I guess he was jealous.

I shouted through the window to Toni that there was no way I could let him in, because Trevor would go mad, and the door was locked. Toni wasn't having any of this. He was coming in one way or the other. So it was decided that he would crawl in through the little kitchen window. I opened up the window and he had one leg and half of his body in when Trevor suddenly appeared. I think he must have been asleep beforehand, otherwise I'm sure he would have been down sooner.

Trevor went wild as soon as he saw what was going on. He started yelling to Toni to "go home and get lost", that he didn't want him in the house. When Trevor went to shove Toni's legs back out, Toni just gave him a push. Unfortunately Trevor had come down the stairs without anything on, so I was a little embarrassed for him. Although I really felt sorry for Trevor, I told him to quit being stupid and either go back to bed or go and get some clothes on. He ignored both suggestions. Trevor was fuming, and wanted us both out of the house.

I don't really know what Toni had thought would happen if he came to Trevor's house. One thing was sure – he was not afraid of Trevor. I believe Toni's original plan was to come and see what I was doing back at Trevor's. All Toni knew was the bad things I'd told him about mine and Trevor's relationship, so I guess he also wanted to check if I was all right. I liked Toni, but he was so unreliable. I needed the security Trevor gave to me. I needed a man close to me and involved in my world all day every day, and that was something I thought Trevor gave to me. I guess they both had different good and bad qualities.

Trevor was really getting irate and threatened to phone the police. We told him to go ahead, and he did. I told him he was behaving stupidly, and that I wanted to finish my drink then pack up my stuff, and assured him that after that we would go. But Trevor wasn't happy about that, as he wanted us out that second. He said he was going to wait in the car until the police came, and that's when I got mad. I wanted him to stick up for himself, maybe even get violent, but all he was doing really was standing back and letting this happen. I told him again not to be so stupid, that this was his house and he had a right to stay there. I told him to stay in the house and sit down, but he insisted on going outside.

Eventually the police came, but I think they were a little annoyed at being called out for such a stupid matter. However, Trevor was in fear for his physical safety from Toni. I put on the real calm cool approach when the police arrived. I sat on Toni's knee drinking my drink as if there was nothing the matter at the house. Trevor was getting neurotic trying to explain that he didn't trust us in the house, was frightened of us and wanted us out that minute. I got annoyed at Trevor. So I decided to try to pull Trevor down a bit and show him up.

I started by talking really nice and calmly to Trevor. In front of the police I told Trevor to calm down, sit down, that he must have taken too many drugs and he didn't really know what he was going on about. I could see him just lose all his fight and give in then. I think the police must have thought that we were just a bunch of escapees from the local nut house. The police told me that Trevor wanted me out and so I made an agreement with them that I would sit and finish my drink then I would pack up and go. The police left and Trevor said he would go and drive around until we were gone. I was glad to see that he put a dressing gown on first.

I was so annoyed at the whole mess, and most of all at Trevor for daring to phone the police on me and ordering me out of the house. I thought if he loved me I could have anybody in the house I wanted in. I started to pack all my stuff up again, and it felt like about the hundredth time I'd done it. I was really pissed off. I'd had quite a lot to drink since coming home by now, so combined with the drink I lost my temper and started to smash up the house.

I started in the bedroom. I pulled the duvet cover off and poured a bottle of bleach all over the bed. Then I picked up his jewelry and a couple of suits, squished them down the toilet and flushed the chain. Toni helped me pack up most of my things from upstairs, then phoned for a taxi. While downstairs waiting for it to arrive I felt pissed off and bored, so I picked up one shoe from each pair I could see and shoved them down the downstairs toilet. Next I got a big pot from the kitchen and went around smashing all the windows in the house.

Now the taxi arrived, so we started loading it up with all my stuff. Next thing we know the police are back at the house, saying a neighbour had phoned them complaining about the noise coming from breaking windows. We were still stood outside the house, and as I was denying there were any broken windows in the house the policeman was looking straight at the kitchen window that had a big hole in. I felt a right cunt.

All of a sudden Trevor arrived on the scene again. I knew I was in for it now. So we all went inside. As the police and Trevor wandered around the house looking at the damage, Toni was getting annoyed at me, telling me: "I told you not to do it." That's all I wanted to hear. Actually he had discouraged me from doing it and he himself had taken no active part in it. Trevor insisted we were arrested and charged with damaging his property, and so we were. I tried to tell the police that Toni didn't do any of the damage, but they insisted that we both had to be taken down and questioned.

When I heard this I took off my shoes and went to attack Trevor with them, so I was quickly put into a car and off we went to Hucknall police station. The police and matrons were brilliant with me. I admitted to doing all the damage out of sheer anger. They weren't too convinced at first. They thought at first that Toni had done most of the damage and that I was taking the blame to keep him out of trouble – or taking the blame because I was afraid of him. I felt bad that I'd gotten Toni involved and arrested and I wanted him to be let out soon. They assured me that he would be released as soon as they found out his last name and address.

I had to take off my tights, have all my property checked, hand in my shoes and coat and was put into a cell. There were only three cells. The matron came along later and gave me a ciggie; but what I really craved for was a drink. I just sat in the cell thinking and regretting what I'd done. I was wishing I was back at Trevor's, curled up in bed asleep. It felt dirty to be sat in an empty cold cell, and there was nothing to do, it was boring. I was just about to get my head down on the bench for a bit of sleep when I heard Toni calling my name.

I wondered where he was at first, then I realised he must have been released and was now outside my cell's thick window. He told me they weren't pressing charges against him, and that he would go to see Trevor to try and persuade him to drop the charges against me and collect my things. I wasn't due to make my statement to the police and then go to court until the following morning. Toni reassured me that he would be back the next day to see if I was OK.

I thought I'd go potty locked in a jail cell with no clean clothes, cosmetics or fags and drink, but I handled it OK. But the more I thought of Trevor having me charged, the angrier

I got. I thought: "How dare he?" Actually I was pissed off at Toni as well. I wished he had never shown up. The next day I made my statement, and told them exactly what I'd done and that I'd done it because I was pissed off at Trevor. The police were a bit curious as to where Toni fit into the whole lot, and they said that they still didn't know his real name or address. I began to wonder what Toni had to hide from me and the police, not telling either his real name or where he lived. I wondered, but I didn't care enough to try to find out.

I didn't have anything to eat all day until in the evening time, when the Matron went to the shop for some sweets and fags, so I ate the sweets. I watched a bit of telly with the Matron. We weren't allowed to sit in the Matron's office, but if we sat in the cell corridor we could see the TV, so I sat there for a while. I had no clean clothes or anything, so I gave the filthy shower a miss. I was convinced that if I went in there I would come out dirtier than when I'd gone in.

In the evening time Toni showed up outside the cell window again. I couldn't see him and it was hard to hear what he was saying, but at least he had come. I didn't think he would be at the court house the following morning, but he insisted that he would. He only stayed a couple of minutes, but I was glad he came. He said that Trevor wouldn't drop the charges, and that my things were in the garage ready to pick up when I got out. Toni didn't tell me, but I later found out that he had gone along to Trevor's parents' pub with a friend of his and a couple of baseball bats and threatened Trevor with them, telling him he was to stay away from me and leave me alone at work. I felt sorry for Trevor when I found out about this because to me Trevor had really done no wrong, except for rightly charging me for smashing up his house.

The next morning I was up at court charged with criminal damage. I felt a right tramp in my dirty clothes, with no make up on. I didn't like people seeing me like this. Toni was at court, and he also had a friend with him. I was a bit nervous and wondered if I would go to prison, but I was just given bail. I was asked where I would be living and I said my Nana's in Sherwood. The reason they wanted to know where I was going to live was because one of the terms of my bail was to not go near Trevor's house. I didn't really care where I would stay; I just said anything so that hopefully I would get out on bail. It worked. I was out on bail with only a condition that I stay away from the house.

Toni and his friend were outside the court waiting for me. I really wished they had left so I could just go somewhere and clean up. I hated being around people when I wasn't dressed nice or looking nice, but I was really grateful they were there because I didn't really know where I was going to go. I had quite a bit of money in my purse, so the first thing we did was grab a taxi, stop off at a shop and get a bottle of vodka, then go and find a hotel. We tried for a room at the hotel where Trevor and I had stayed. It was small and quiet and, more importantly, it was very clean. I went inside while Toni and his friend stayed in the taxi. I don't think the proprietors remembered me, and they gave me a double room.

I gave Toni and his friend some money for the taxi and told them to go and get my things out of Trevor's garage, while I went up into the room and had a drink. Toni and his friend returned a while later with all my stuff packed up in a jumbled mess. I didn't unpack much stuff, just the things I would need to get ready to go out to work that evening.

We spent a while just sitting around talking, and me drinking. I was feeling a bit worried about giving the court house my Nana's address, as I was actually staying at a hotel. I worried that if was arrested that night I would be in trouble. I wondered if I dared ask my Nana if I could stay with her. I would have liked to, I loved the purity and simplicity of her life and I thought I could do with a break. I decided that I would phone her, tell her I was in a bit of trouble, and that I would go over and talk to her about it.

I went along for a bath and Toni and his friend left, Toni saying that he would meet me on the beat after work was finished. I phoned my Nana, and told her I was in trouble and

I was going over in the evening to talk to her about it. She didn't seem too pleased, but she agreed. I phoned a taxi to take me to my Nana's. It was still too early for work, so I planned to come back to the hotel before either going to work or packing my stuff back up and going to stay with my Nana again.

I felt very uncomfortable at my Nana's house. She was in one of her high and mighty moods. She thought I looked quite rough like I wasn't taking care of myself, and kept asking me why I had left her house in the first place. I told her I had just wanted a change, but now I was in trouble and needed somewhere to stay. She said there was no way I could stay there, and asked me if I was prostituting myself. I told her I was.

She was worried that my friends might come around and cause trouble. "What friends?", I wanted to know. Nana didn't like the clothes I was wearing either, like my short skirts and revealing tops. She wondered what the neighbours would think. I was very annoyed with her attitude. I thought if she loved me like she claimed she loved all us three girls, then why wouldn't she let me stay with her for a while? I just got annoyed with her, walked out of the room we were sitting in, phoned myself a taxi and sat on the stairs waiting for it to come. I didn't say goodbye to her when I left, but she shouted it to me.

I felt absolutely down in the dumps. I wondered why I was such a hard person to love, as there had never been enough people around in my life to love me, I think that is what I craved most in life. I decided I'd just have to stay at the hotel and hope I wasn't arrested before I was to appear in court again. When I got back to the hotel, things changed again. As soon as I walked in the door, the lady that owned the place said she wanted me out. I thought, what the hell is going on here? She said she had been up to my room and it was a complete mess and that she didn't appreciate me spending all afternoon sat up there drinking with two Black men.

I decided from that statement that she, like a lot of other people, was colour prejudiced, and that that pissed me off.

She had no reason to go into my room except to be nosy, and that also pissed me off. I told her I wasn't leaving, because I had paid for a night's stay. She then said that she had overheard my telephone conversation and heard that I was in trouble with the police, and that she would phone them if I didn't leave. I was defeated. God, I wanted to rant and rave that I was not a bad person, and that I would cause no trouble while staying there. Sometimes I think people's prejudices were un-called for. Wow, I wanted to scream, what a mess I'd gotten myself into again.

I packed up my things again, phoned a taxi and went out looking for another hotel. I went to quite a few around the beat areas before I found one with a room. It was a bit of a dive, really grotty looking and cheap. I really didn't like the hotel, but I was just glad I'd at last found a room to sleep in. I booked a double room again, because I figured Toni would be staying with me. I paid the bill, put my things in the room and went out to work. I didn't need a taxi to take me there, because the hotel was right on the beat. I got a punter right outside the hotel.

I worked all night until fifteen minutes before the time I was due to meet Toni at the previous hotel. When Toni found out that I'd been kicked out he was fuming. He wanted to confront the proprietors and he tried to call them out, but they just ignored us and wouldn't open the door. It was cold out and I had had enough already that day, so I told him to forget it. We walked to the other hotel. It was about midnight when we arrived and we found that the outside door was locked, so had to ring the bell for someone to open it.

More trouble was yet to come. As soon as the owner, who had come to let me in, saw Toni she said he couldn't stay. I thought she was mad at first, and asked her why. She said that because it was classed as a single stay. I thought this was crazy. I had paid for a double room with a double bed in it, so it was obvious that there would be two people to sleep there that night. This was the final straw. I even got mad at

Toni. I told him to piss off and never come back to see me. I was so upset I wanted to cry. I never really liked being by myself overnight, and when it was caused by something stupid it got me angry.

Toni said "stay cool", that it didn't matter, and that he would go home and see me in the morning. But it wasn't OK. Today had been a bad day and I'd had enough. I went up to my room and cried. I was so fed up. I didn't even think of calling Trevor, but I really wanted to talk to my mother but couldn't. I had really had enough. I got my bottle of vodka out and sat drinking and crying. I was looking at the photos of my mother and brothers and that made me more depressed. I always want my mother when I am upset or lonely. I wanted to be with them. I wanted to end my life, and I wanted someone to come along and take away all of my problems. I don't know which one I wanted most.

I could hear Toni outside the window shouting to see if I was going to be all right there all night by myself. I went to the window and told him it didn't matter if I was OK, because I didn't want to live anymore anyway. I sat at the window talking to him, which made me feel even more sorry for myself. By now I was really getting hysterical, and drinking the vodka neat. I told Toni to go away, and came from the window. I went into my luggage and got out a packet of razor blades, sat on the bed and cut both of my wrists. I was really going bananas in the room. I couldn't figure out what I wanted to do. I wished for the courage to kill myself, but I didn't have it.

I could hear that Toni was in the hotel now. I started to panic. Obviously he had got the woman to let him in for a moment, and now he was at the door wanting to come in. In a way I wanted to open the door and let him in to be with me, but in another way I just wanted to be left alone. I told him again to go away. Now he was getting angry. He yelled for the woman to get up the stairs and open the door because he thought I was going to commit suicide. The woman raced up the stairs and opened the door. Toni went bananas when he saw what I had done to myself. They were pretty deep cuts and a lot of blood around, and I think he thought it was a lot worse than it really was. He called me all the stupid cunts under the sun. He wanted to know why I had done it. He was yelling at me, and that made me cry even more. Why did he have to yell?

He screamed to the woman to get an ambulance but I begged her not to, saying it was OK, I just needed a plaster, but Toni wasn't having any of it. He wanted me to go to the hospital. He wrapped my arms up in towels and carried me down the stairs to wait for the ambulance. When it got there I started kicking up a fuss, saying I wasn't going without him, but he promised he would come too. He didn't wait for the attendants to come in; he just took me out to them. I got in and away we went. They asked me what was the matter, but I didn't want to talk to them so I just ignored them. Toni told them that I was just a bit depressed, and was still telling me how stupid I was. But I gave him a sharp look and so he stopped.

When we got to the hospital the attendants took me through to emergency to wait to be stitched up. I wasn't taken to the waiting room, just a side corridor and sat on a stretcher. They asked me my name and I told them it was Lisa Lomax. I don't know why I didn't tell them my real name. I was waiting ages to be stitched up, and Toni wasn't around. A while later a nurse came along and started to talk to me. She asked if I had come with anyone, and I said about Toni being here with me. She said she would go to get him to sit with me until the doctor was ready. But she came back a few minutes later and said that there was no Toni waiting around the hospital.

That really put me right down again. I wondered how could he make me come here, then piss off on me. But previously when I'd thought badly of him he had turned out OK. I thought maybe he would show up later, and he did, when the doctor was stitching me up. I was so happy to see him, and smiled for the first time that day. He just said that he'd been wandering around the place for a while. He was in an OK mood now, but he asked me never to do it again because it had frightened him a bit. When I was stitched up, Toni and I went back to the hotel. I think the woman who owned it was feeling a bit bad, but still a bit pissed off. She asked if I was OK and said I could still stay there that night, but she would like me to go the next day.

Toni stayed for a while to give me a few lectures. He said things would be all right in the morning. He made a point of pouring my bottle of booze down the sink, which I was annoyed about, but I knew there was plenty more where that came from so really it was no big deal. Toni came back the next morning. I felt really rotten, and didn't feel like moving hotels again. I sat down in the lounge for a while, as Toni phoned around and found a hotel close by with a single room. I had trouble carrying all the stuff up to my room because it was hurting my arms where they'd been cut, so the owner's daughter helped me up with them.

I was glad for the move once I had unpacked a few things. This place was much more comfortable. The room was spotless and pretty looking – small – the bathroom was the same. Because I'd hardly slept the night before, I decided to wait until Toni came back, have a drink and a bath then go to bed for a kip. Toni said he'd come back later, before I went out to work. I had more than one drink though! I think I would have downed the whole half bottle before I went to sleep, but I knew I needed some to wake up to. I wasn't drunk, just dying to sleep. I woke at about four in the afternoon and had another bath and washed my hair.

I'd done my nails and dried my hair, and had half my make up on when Toni came around. I needed another bottle of vodka, so when I was dressed and ready we went to the shops. We got another full bottle, some mix and some sweets. After we came out he threatened to go back and warn the cashier not to serve me again because I was under age, but he didn't. We went back to the hotel and I had a few more drinks, and we messed around having a laugh and a joke. He was in a good mood. Later on we phoned for a taxi and I went to work.

Toni stayed around the beat until my first customer came around, then he went away. Sometimes he was very overpowering, and wanting to rule my life like a husband or boyfriend would. Other times he was the complete opposite. It was like he knew everything about me, but I never knew anything about him. Apart from doing weight training at the gym, I never knew what he got up to. Sometimes I was very unsure as to what our relationship was — other times I was sure that I was happy to just be his friend — nothing more. Other times he was happy with things that way. Later on that evening, Toni came to see me at work, and while we were talking, Trevor drove around. I saw his car coming, so when he went past Toni stuck up his fingers and shouted obscenities at him. I didn't bother. I was still mad at Trevor so I didn't even give a reaction.

I stayed in this hotel for a couple of weeks. I continued to work every night, then spend all of the money on clothes, booze and little knick-knacks. I didn't see much of Toni at all; I guess he just drifted away. I don't think I was living my life at this time; I was just existing in a world of booze and prostitution. I continued to go into the Fosters pub and drink and talk to Hans and Neil. Hans wanted to go to bed with me, but I didn't fancy him in that way. Also, I knew he had a girlfriend. I also quite liked talking to Neil who worked there. He seemed like a good guy, and I could sit and talk to him for ages and he would just sit there and listen and listen, but he never got fed up of me waffling away to him, so he made me feel at ease.

One night I decided to try to see Trevor again. Apart from seeing him driving around the beat, or seeing him in the pub, I hadn't had any contact with him since I got charged with the criminal damage. I felt like going to see him, and being with someone I thought cared about me. I asked the driver to pass the house to see if he was home, but he wasn't. I was sad he wasn't there; I really wanted to see him. I got some paper off the driver, scribbled a note saying I'd been looking for him, and put it in the letterbox. I figured I'd better get back to the hostel, but on the way there I decided to go look to see if he was at the pub, which he was. I saw his car parked outside, and I felt relieved. I wondered if maybe he had some other woman there with him? But I wasn't bothered, all knew was I wanted to be with him.

When he opened the pub door he gave me one of his full smiles – eyes, teeth, everything. He was surprised to see me. He gave me money for the taxi and we went into the pub. I was pleased to see he was alone. I don't know if he was just closing up, or if he was sitting there by himself. I told him I'd had a bad night, and he made me feel secure and loved immediately. We had quite a talk that night, and sat there playing the jukebox and drinking for hours. We talked about our feelings for each other, something we rarely did apart from if we argued. I always found it difficult to talk about, or even show my feelings. I used to try, but I felt I never came across the way I wanted to.

He wanted to know why I didn't go out and find someone better then him? He always put himself down when talking of why we stayed together. I think he meant a younger, more handsome guy. But I'd gone beyond just going for the guys because they looked good. I wanted a man who had a mind of his own. I wanted a man who could love and understand me. I wanted to love a man for his inside qualities. Trevor was not ugly, he was just not handsome. He knew I liked nice-looking men sometimes. I never had any problem getting any man if I wanted him, he knew that too. But I knew he had other girls when I wasn't around.

That night ended up feeling like one of the first nights we met and fell in love. We didn't go home that night, and I didn't bother calling the hostel. We made love next to the fire, on the floor of the pub, and that's where we slept. I kept waking him up, wanting to be cuddled and caressed, but he was tired, and just kept falling back to sleep. As we lay there in the morning I had an awful feeling about losing him. I did not want to lose our togetherness when I felt nice and secure, lying there next to him. I often wondered why he bothered with me, because I felt I treated him very badly at times.

That moment as we lay on the floor I decided I wanted to marry him. I needed to feel a bond between us. The chance of me having a baby seemed slim now, so I wanted to get married to him. He was still pretty sleepy, but I told him: "Let's get married." He looked at me as if to say: "Did I hear you right?" Then as easily as I suggested it, he said "OK". I didn't believe him though. I thought maybe he assumed I was joking about it. So for the next fifteen minutes I never shut up about it – telling him how serious I was and how I wanted to go out that day to see when we could get married. We got up and bathed and dressed, and I had a couple of drinks. We then left, as the cleaner was due in very soon.

We went into town, and I said to him I wanted him to buy me a ring. He said that he didn't have very much money on him, and that I didn't need one. I usually got what I wanted when I wanted it, so I was angry that we would not be shopping for a ring that morning. Mind you, I figured I'd get it another time, so I wasn't too bothered. After our coffees we went around to about five different registry offices. We were at it for ages, going from one to the other, trying to find out when was the earliest we could get married. We gave up in the end.

I was dying for a drink, but I didn't want to go into anywhere, because I felt scruffy and unclean still in yesterday's clothes, and with my hair not done. So we got a bottle and went back to the house. I couldn't believe how neat and tidy it looked without all my stuff scattered here and there. I figured he wasn't spending too much time at home. Apart from a few little things I'd left at the house, there was nothing there to say it was still my home. But it felt like my home, and I felt comfortable there. I was tired from hardly having any sleep the night before, and trekking here and there all morning, so I sat and dozed for a while.

Trevor went out and got some chips, which I ate a few of. I phoned my mom and had a good talk with her. Later on we started to make love on the couch, and the phone rang. I thought it might be my mother so I wanted to answer it, but Trevor picked up the receiver and put it straight back down again. I was a bit pissed off about that, as I had to get back to the hostel soon, and God knows when I'd get to talk to my mom again. We were still on the couch making love when someone started knocking on the front door. Trevor told me to keep quiet, as he didn't want to answer it. Then I began to wonder who it was. I assumed it was another girlfriend of his, so I went mad. We had a massive row and I stormed back to the hostel.

I was in a real state when I got in. One of the girls came up with me to see if I was OK, then she left. I felt that once again everything had gone wrong. I decided to take an overdose. I don't know if I wanted to die that night, or if I just wanted to make myself ill so I could avoid meeting Trevor tomorrow, but I went and downed every pill I could find in my room. There were only about 40 soluble aspirin and 40 Feminax painkillers, but it was enough to make me very poorly for the next two days. I didn't bother dissolving the aspirin; I just downed them all whole. I didn't feel anything at all, I was just knackered and wanting to get into bed and sleep. I had a fag, turned the radio on low, and went to sleep.

One of the staff came and checked up on me later, but I was out for the count and didn't hear her. She saw the empty pill boxes in the sink, but didn't bother to wake me because she knew I'd be awake soon enough with the pains. Sure enough the pains woke me up. Luckily I had some fluid in my stomach so that helped a bit, but I felt so poorly I was crying. I kept slipping back to sleep, then waking up having to drink glasses and glasses of water so I'd at least have something to throw up. I felt like I'd swallowed acid or poison. My stomach wanted to explode.

The next day I stayed in bed until the early afternoon. I still felt like I was half-dead, but the pains and vomiting were over. I didn't drink any booze that day. I didn't think I could stomach it. I put on my fuzzy pyjamas and staggered downstairs to doss in front of the telly. I wasn't really watching it, I just wanted to be around people. So, I lay on the couch feeling like I wanted to crawl into a hole and die, I felt so awful.

Trevor phoned that afternoon. I really didn't want to talk to him, I just wanted to be left alone. He was not very amused. He wanted to know what had happened to yesterday's ideas of love and marriage. I think he thought I was trying to avoid him, because he had never known me to be ill before except the time I was struck with stomach cramps, and I suppose he thought I was telling him I was ill to avoid him.

I was still dozing on the couch in the evening time. I felt a bit better by then. I'd managed to have some hot cups of tea and went into the dining room and had some tea. At about six that night the CID visited the hostel. When the staff called me into the office to see them I thought they had breached my bail so I started to panic a bit, but the staff assured me they hadn't. So I went into the office to see them. There were two CID but I've never met them before. I was very curious as to what they wanted, then they told me:

While working on the beat, I'd been approached by a Rastafarian man. When I refused his advances he'd threatened to sew my vagina up, and told me he'd be back to do it some day soon. I'd never reported this incident, but I think I'd mentioned it to one or two of the other girls working in my area. The CID reckoned I knew who the guy is and wanted to know his name. I told them I know nothing of the guy except of that one incident. The officers were not happy with this reply, and tried to insist I knew who he was. Then they gave me a sob story about how he had attacked and raped another girl at work. I wasn't too sure whether or not to believe this, but in a way, that was irrelevant. I simply didn't know what they wanted to know.

Then they gave me a proposition. If I gave them the guy's name, I could have a few weeks on the beat with no arrests from the Vice squad. That sounded all right, but arrests didn't bother me in the slightest really, and it wasn't as if I was picked up every night, so really I wasn't interested in their proposition. But to get them off my back I told them that maybe if I was to take the night off work I could go sit in the Black clubs and find out the guy's name for them. In other words, if they let me have at least six weeks on the beat with no fear of arrests, and give me one night's pay, maybe I could come up with a name. They seemed to agree with that, but still insisted I was protecting him. They even tried to make me feel guilty, by telling me I was being unfair to the other girls by allowing the guy to roam around attacking women. I didn't know his name, so the guilt trip didn't work at all. I wondered why they really had come to see me.

I saw Toni a few times and he took me out. He drifted in and out of my life. I think he was just interested in the work of a prostitute, and wanted to turn me into a good girl. I don't even know what kind of good girl, because he was always there ready to give me all the drinks I wanted, so to him it was OK for me to drink but not to work.

The Homicide

I now want to explain how the things that happened to me, both as a child and when I came back to Nottingham and got involved in prostitution, built up to the night I killed Trevor. I began working as a prostitute for the money. I enjoyed the money, but I hated the men. I did not stop prostitution, because I wanted to remain independent. But I wanted to stop it, because I did not like it. I always wondered why I did not like men for boyfriends. When I was in Canada I slept around with a lot of men, but I hardly got any sexual pleasure out it. The more I became aware that I did not like men in a sexual way, the more I slept with them, trying to like it, and trying to hide from the world what I felt inside. But the more sex I had with men the more I hated them as boyfriends.

While in Canada I was very vulnerable, and one time while on AWOL from a home I got myself into a situation where pornographic photos were taken of my best friend and me. When I knew these pictures were circulating, I felt very much used and ashamed of them. When confronted by investigators, I was at first very keen to see that the pictures were found and the men responsible taken to court. But I changed my mind, because I did not want to be humiliated by these men or the pictures any more, and just wanted to forget about them. I was 14 at the time.

Another time in Canada when I was 15 I was on AWOL again when a man who seemed all right picked me up. I went back to his place with him and was offered two beers and two tablets, which I took. I believe that there were more tablets in the drink. I remember falling over, and remember keeping waking up with this man doing things sexually to me. I woke up two days later, and the man took me and dumped me in an alleyway. I could hardly walk, but I got to a shop where someone phoned a taxi for me.

I took the taxi to the truck stop where my two friends Bryan and Lori worked. These two friends were girlfriend and boyfriend. When I got there they were shocked at the state I was in and wanted to take me to hospital, but I did not want to go because I was on the run. Lori helped me into the shower there and cleaned me up a bit, because there was blood running down me. It was time for Bryan to go off duty, so he took me back to their apartment, where I was invited to stay until I decided what to do.

Bryan helped me get into something of Lori's and put me on the couch to sleep, because I was still very heavily drugged. I woke up with Bryan fondling me. I could not fight against him because I was too weak, and could hardly think straight. He started to have intercourse with me and I fell back to sleep. When I woke up I pretended nothing had happened, and as soon as I was well the next day I left to go up north to get away from the city. Months later I saw someone from the Rape Crisis Centre because how these men used my body when I was in such a drugged condition really bothered me, and not knowing exactly what they did bothered me even more.

In about November 1985, whilst I was working as a prostitute in Nottingham and living with Trevor, though still very gullible, I was confronted by a man who made out that he could not speak properly, but I understood that he wanted me to go with him for business. I got into his car and went to a house where I thought I was going into to have business with him. I walked into what I thought was the living room, which turned out to have nothing in it but a mattress. The door was locked behind me, and two other men came out of another room or a closet. One of them pulled out a pair of scissors from his trousers, and then I was raped one after the other by the three men. I was very frightened and did not fight as I was in fear of my life.

Afterwards I was driven into town, where I took a taxi straight home. I became very upset, and felt used. As soon as I was home I phoned Trevor, not telling him what had happened, just asking him to came home straight away. He said he would come home, but he did not turn up for about three hours. I phoned my Mum and told her about it, but when Trevor came home I would not discuss it with him, because I felt hurt that he did not come home when I needed him. I did not report the rape to the police because I did not want to feel more embarrassed telling them, and I thought that maybe they would think it was my fault because I got in the car and I went into the house. A while after the rape I was visited by the police, who took me down to the police station to make statements. The only way I think they knew is because I had told some of the other girls working in my area to watch out for them. After the rape I wanted to quit working, but it was my income and the only way I knew how to make money.

Trevor was not sadistic or perverted any more than any other man. But I hated him sexually, just the same as I hated the next man. I enjoyed affection from him and enjoyed sleeping in the same bed as him, but I could not stand sex with him or anyone else. I wanted a father/brother relationship with him. I loved him and wanted to make him happy, and wanted to enjoy sex with him, and even though I tried I couldn't. Sometimes I would feel very sick inside when I gave into him and let him have sex with me. I would feel very mixed up inside and get very upset. I told my mother about this because I thought I wasn't normal, but no advice my mother could give me helped in any way.

When I refused Trevor sex, sometimes he would force me to do it, saying, "Little girls had to pay for what they did wrong," and treating and talking to me as if I were a child that had done something wrong. This would leave me feeling even more cold towards him and hating him violating my body. Other times he would make me tell him what I had done for my clients that night, and he would tell me I was a slag and that I enjoyed having sex with my clients.

Trevor and I would never talk about any problems we had, we just fought or did not speak. On the night of my crime I was terrified of having sex with him. When he took his clothes off I knew what was coming, and I could not bring myself to have sex with him once more. I thought if I killed him all our problems would be over, that the whole situation would be over, and I would not have to give him myself.

I feel able to talk about my crime more now than when I had the chance to at my trial. This leaves me with frustrated feelings that maybe if had spoken up and told my story to a jury, I may not have ended up with a life sentence. I was also ashamed of some of the things in my life that I am no longer ashamed of and am able to discuss. Even with my solicitor I was not able to talk openly about things to him. I know it is my own fault, but I feel cheated. Being young and confused at the time of my trial, I was not able to speak up for myself like I can now. Sometimes I think the courts take advantage of the kind of situation I was in. I want to speak up and defend myself.

In my police statement I said that Trevor and I had agreed to live together, but not have sex. That is not true. There was no arrangement made or discussed, but I had refused to have sex with him for four days prior to my arrest. I loved Trevor, but not in a sexual way. I said in my police statement that Trevor had seen I had cut my wrists. That is not true. If he had seen them he would have become very upset, like he did the last time I cut my wrists at his house. Or he may have become violent towards me. I said in my police statement that I took two knives upstairs to cut my wrists and to protect myself. That is not true. I took them upstairs to cut my wrists. Nowhere in my mind was there a thought to frighten or hurt Trevor with them.

I did not plan to kill my boyfriend while he was away driving his son home. It was unfortunate that I am someone who cuts up when things in my life are going wrong. The most unfortunate part is that I had a weapon in my hands from cutting up when I was confronted with a situation that I could not handle at the time.

I had been released from Risley, where I had spent three weeks for prostitution offenses and assault, four days before he died. I was happy to be back living with Trevor, but I was not happy going back into the same situation as before: prostitution, drinking, sexual problems, communication problems, and the fighting. I refused him sex every night since I was back. I could not bring myself to have sex with him any more. He was not happy with that, so there was tension between us. I was very worried about the situation, because I knew that sooner or later I would have to have sex with him, either by giving in again or by force.

On the night of my crime, Trevor came home from work as usual about 5p.m. We did not speak much, but he was curious as to why the police had been to our house that day. The truth is that my mother had called them from Canada and asked them to come round, because I had been telling her how scared I was from his increasing violence towards me, and that someone was going to get hurt. Trevor left the house in a grumpy mood. Later on he had a taxi called to the house to take me to work. I went to work, took one client, and came home. I had a taxi take me back to my work area but I had no change, so we both arranged to go into a pub to have a drink and get change to pay him. I was sat having a drink with the driver when Trevor and his son came into the pub. I immediately felt the bad vibes from Trevor, but I could not explain to him why I was in there because there was a lot of people around, and Trevor was distant.

The taxi driver left my company and Trevor came over. After a few sarcastic remarks Trevor, his son, and a friend of Trevor's and mine left the pub and headed out to the car to go on to another pub. While getting into the car, there was a suggestion that they should gang bang me. The thought frightened me. Trevor did not usually speak like that in front of people, and I was worried because I did not know what the three of them, after a few drinks, were capable of. Also, Trevor wanted me to sit in the back of the car, which was very strange.

I laughed the remark off and got into the car. I just stayed quiet, so maybe they would forget about me being there. We went on to another pub. There was an uneasy feeling between Trevor and I. He made some sarcastic remarks about how he thought I wanted to sleep with his son and told us to go home together, and he told his son since I had refused him sex the night before. This made me feel bad, as he was letting me know that he was cross. I began worrying how the night was going to end up. I started to get nerves in my stomach and told his son I could not drink my drink, that I did not want it.

Trevor, his son and myself left the pub and went home. They wanted to watch TV, but I wanted to listen to music. So they stayed downstairs in front of the TV, and I went upstairs onto the landing to listen to music. Some time later Trevor shouted up to me that he was going out to drive his son home.

He left, and straight away I started to worry about what

was going to happen when he came home. I knew he was cross that I had been sitting in the pub with a man and not out working, and I knew he was cross that I would not let him have sex with me, so I knew that there was bound to be trouble. I did not want to have sex with him, and I did not want to get beaten up. I did not know what to do.

I decided that I would cut up, thinking that if I did he would take me to hospital for stitches, and then he would not demand sex or hit me. I started to cut my wrists, then I heard him coming. I got frightened and wondered if I had done the right thing, so I turned my arm down so he could not see if he came upstairs, and I don't remember if I had the knives or not, but I know at least one of them was still near me. I put on a Marvin Gaye tape to try to relax myself.

He came straight up the stairs and passed me to go into the bedroom. I felt relieved because I thought he was going to bed, but a couple of minutes later he came out of the bedroom wearing only his open shirt. I knew straight away that he wanted sex. I hated it, and could not bring myself to give into his demands any more. He came and laid right beside me, so that I could see the lower part of his body. Neither of us said anything, so there was an awkward silence.

I was terrified of letting him have sex by being forced, so I decided then and there that the easiest way out of the situation was to kill him or me. I did not want to kill him because I loved him, and I believed he loved me, but I could not carry on with that evening, or the whole life we had together. I was frightened to do it, and thought that maybe I couldn't, so I sat there for a couple of minutes, psyching myself up for it and just telling myself that I had to. Very quickly I turned around, shutting my eyes, and threw myself on top of him with the knife in my hand to stab him.

I sat back not believing it. Trevor stood up all shocked, and I moved back. He said "Oh! God!" then turned around and fell backwards onto the mirror, landing on the floor. I started yelling at him, saying why did he let me do it, and telling him he better not die, and that I did it because I loved him. Then when I realised he was dying I started to cry a lot, wanting him well again. I held him and cuddled him, and just kept asking him not to die. I did not want to leave him. I don't know how long after, but he stopped breathing loud so I thought he was dead. My instant thought was to get someone into the house to see him. I ran out of the house and went out into the street. A man in a car came along and I stopped him and shouted for him to come into the house.

After that, things are pretty hazy.

Womanly Wise

I'm not ever going to get my childhood back.
Well, not going to be able to relive it how it was
Or how I would have liked it to have been.
But one thing's for sure
I'm determined to remember it
And face what I couldn't face then.

You see, my mind has lots of empty spaces
Those are the times I believe I went to noddy land
Where I still go now, when things aren't nice.

I have clips, a flash here and there
But big, big empty spaces.
I don't do a lot of conscious work on the regaining of my
childhood.
I believe in the power of the mind
That what I need to know, when I need to know
It will come back to me.

I'm twenty-seven now
And when my physical self is free
From these bars and walls
I shall live childishly and adolescent wildly
And womanly wise.

What does it mean?

What does it mean?
Oh, it can mean all sorts of things.
Like eating a lettuce leaf
While trying to control a craving.

A craving for what?
Bad food.
Every bite that feeds me guilt.
My comforter, my enemy
Food.

I know it's hard for you to believe
Or even imagine
I've done it all.
Yes, all of those disgusting things
You've read about them
Maybe seen something on the TV
Or even experienced something similar.

Retching in the toilet bowl
Aching and anxious
Waiting to see it drop in the toilet
The first thing eaten
The beginning and ending of another binge
Now I'm back in control.

Yes, me once again.
In control of my personal nightmare.
I'm me . . . as how you see me.

What you see, the physical me
Well, it doesn't tell you much
Oh, but it could be seen if searched for
Some proof I do those disgusting things.

In and amongst the others
Self-abusive gashes
Up and down my arms.

Did I really do that?
Just to avoid a weekly weigh
Cut my wrists and enter solitary confinement
Ashamed of my sinning
My loss of control?

This was before regular vomits
Days without food, true fasts
Then secretly scoffing, watch my belly swell.
Then curl up on the bed
So uncomfortable, so depressed.

I guess I blew my true fast the day I slit my wrists.
I can't even remember which are the scars.
Ashamed and suicidal
What would people think?
Am I crazy?
Lost it completely?
Can you really believe it?

Me, quiet and mysterious
They call me the pretty, skinny girl
They don't know me
Me who longs to be normal
Not alienated from people.

Why did you ask me what it means?
It's a damn obsession, a habit.
I can't get it out of me.

Please don't ask me again.

Holloway
April 1994

POST Comment

Emma: The case for a fresh appraisal

WAS it murder — or should Emma Humphreys have been convicted of the lesser offence of manslaughter?

What is not in dispute is that Emma, then aged 17, killed the boyfriend she both loved and loathed.

She says Trevor Armitage teased her about her attempts to slash her wrists. She feared he was about to hit her. And he allegedly threatened her with gang rape.

Jailed prostitute to appeal over murder in 1985

By Caroline Davies

THE case of a former prostitute who murdered her boyfriend is to be heard by the Court of Appeal this week, 10 years after she was convicted.

Emma Humphreys, now 27, is to introduce new evidence on the grounds of provocation after a campaign by the pressure group Justice for Women, which took up her case two-and-a-half years ago.

In the wake of other appeals centred on the issue of violence suffered by women at the hands of their male partners, campaigners — including the actress Julie Christie and the Labour MP Glenda Jackson — hope she will be released after Thursday's hearing.

She was convicted at Nottingham Crown Court in 1985 ment and at the same time granted her leave to appeal.

During her original trial, Humphreys, then 17, gave no evidence. Today, campaigners claim the court was not sufficiently well informed about the provocation she had suffered during her life.

She was born in Dolgellau, in Wales, but her parents divorced and her mother, an alcoholic, married a Canadian oil worker and moved the family to Canada.

Ms Bindel said a 200-page dossier on her life would be submitted to the court including details of violence inflicted by her stepfather. It tells how she began working as a prostitute aged just 13, developed a drink problem and anorexia, and attempted suicide in her early teens.

She was placed in care in

Dear Jud free me

KILLER Emma Humphreys y day pleaded for her freedom spending 10 years in jail for bing her live-in lover throug heart.

In an emotional letter begi "Dear Judges" she asked the A Court to release her from "a life of

The 27-year-old blonde was a age prostitute when she was con at Nottingham for killing Trevor tage, 33. She claimed he was ab rape her.

Release hope for woman who killed

**Duncan Campbell
Crime Correspondent**

COURT of Appeal judges yesterday gave a strong indication that Emma Humphreys, jailed for life for killing her violent lover, will be freed when they deliver their judgment next Friday.

Humphreys, aged 27, was convicted at Nottingham crown court in December 1985 of murdering Kevin Armitage, aged 33. She was a teenage prostitute living with Mr Armitage when she stabbed him in the heart in February 1985 at his Nottingham home. She has appealed against her conviction on the grounds that the trial judge had not properly directed the jury on the issue of provocation.

Yesterday Lord Justice Hirst, sitting with Mr Justice Kay and Mr Justice Cazalet, said: "If we allow this appeal we substitute a verdict of manslaughter for one of murder, at which point there will be a debate about sentence. It would be helpful if we have a prison report and prison medical report."

Lord Hirst told Helen Grindrod QC, counsel for Humphreys, that no final decision had yet been made.

No request was made for bail for Humphreys, who was in court. If released, she will stay in a residential home in the South and receive counselling for up to two years.

She was born in Dolgellau, Gwynedd, and brought up in Canada and Nottingham. She was a prostitute in Canada at 13, had been in a series of institutions and suffered violence at the hands of her stepfather and her lover, the court has heard.

John Milmo QC, contesting the appeal for the crown, said Humphreys had never been denied the opportunity to put her past life in evidence.

Helen Grindrod QC, for Humphreys, said: "Trevor Armitage had, an hour before, threatened this girl with a 'gang rape'. She was in a vulnerable state. She knew he wanted to have sex with her."

The history of Mr Armitage's provocative behaviour should have been highlighted for the jurors, she said. The trial judge had restricted them to considering the provocation immediately before the killing. Mr Justice Kay said: "Not many people find themselves with a life history that this girl had."

After the hearing, Julie Bindel of Justice for Women, said the group was very optimistic about the result.

Chanting crowds demand release of form

Woman who killed violent lover at 16 appeals for freedom

BY RICHARD DUCE

A FORMER teenage prostitute was wrongly convicted of murdering her boyfriend ten years ago because the trial judge stopped the jury from considering his history of violence, the Court of Appeal was told yesterday.

The case of Emma Humphreys, 27, is regarded by women's groups and some lawyers as a classic example of a killing in which the defence of provocation is justified. Outside, the court yesterday crowds of women chanted slogans calling for her release.

Humphreys, then aged 16, stabbed Trevor Armitage, 33, in the chest at their home in Nottingham. She claims that she feared another of his regular beatings and that Armitage planned to rape her.

Helen Grindrod, QC, opening the appeal, said the trial judge should have asked the jury to take into account the history of violent behaviour by Armitage. Instead of emphasising the cumulative provocation over the six months of the girl's relationship with Armitage, Mr Justice Jones had restricted the jury at Nottingham Crown Court to considering the prov-

Emma Humphreys

ocation immediately before the killing, Mrs Grindrod said.

The jury did not accept her defence of manslaughter on the ground of provocation and Humphreys was convicted of murder. She was sentenced to be detained at Her Majesty's pleasure.

In April 1985, without taking legal advice, she signed a document giving up her right to appeal. She changed her mind after reading the case of Kiranjit Ahluwalia, who was jailed for killing her husband but freed after a retrial when the extent of his violence became known.

Mrs Grindrod said Humphreys's parents separated when she was five and she was taken to Canada, where her mother remarried. Both mother and stepfather were also alcoholics. At the age of 13 she had become a prostitute and by 16 had had a history of antisocial behaviour, included shoplifting and alcohol abuse.

Humphreys returned to Britain in 1983, and met Armitage in September 1984 when she was picked up by him while working as a prostitute. Although he wanted her to carry on as a prostitute, he called her "a dirty tramp" and would often beat her.

On the night of his death Armitage had got drunk in the company of three men, including his son, and suggested they should all have sex together with Humphreys. Later she attempted to slash her wrists with a knife.

Armitage taunted her for having made a "pathetic" attempt to cut her wrists. Then, fearful the she might be beaten and raped, Humphreys picked up a knife and stabbed him, penetrating his heart and killing him.

The case continues.

Inside

Emma Humphreys . . . appeal judgment due next Friday

I WANT TO BE FREE

EXPRESS REPORTER

lease, I beg you, don't send me back to rison. I was 10 years old when I first an away from home. I was 12 years old n Canada when I again started to run way and the first few times I just got eturned to my home.

"I took a drastic step one day. I used ny dinner money to buy azor blades. Sat in the sch ut my wrists for the first ne took a little notice a asn't sent back home.

THE TIMES F...

ute in provocation case

...Humphreys protesting outside the Court of Appeal

'I decided one day that the first man I

● Emma Humphries — has won right to appeal

NOTTINGHAM vice girl Emma Humphries who killed her violent boyfriend ten years ago could finally win her freedom next month.

Emma was found guilty of murdering Trevor Armitage when she was just 17.

Now she has won the first round — the right to appeal — in a decade-long campaign against the conviction. The appeal will be heard at the High Court in London on June 26.

By LIZ CARTWRIGHT

It was in 1985 that she was imprisoned for an indefinite term at Nottingham Crown Court for killing 33-year-old "toffee figure" boyfriend to death.

The judge quashed the notice.

Julie Bindel, spokeswoman for Justice for Women, said: "Everybody is rooting for Emma, apart from the Home Office which is deeply embarrassed about the case."

"Even the most sometimes unsympathetic people who think conviction is absurd, want to...

BATTLING: Emma hopes to win murder appeal

End of 10-year hell in sight

Prisoner hopes to win her freedom

■ By Beverly Davies

A DOLGELLAU-BORN woman, jailed 10 years ago for killing her violent partner, is hoping to win her freedom in the Court of Appeal next week.

Emma Humphreys was just 17 when she killed her 33-year-old boyfriend Trevor Armitage with a single stab wound.

Her defence of manslaughter at Nottingham Crown Court in December 1985, on the grounds of provocation, failed, despite supporting evidence by psychiatrist Dr Michael Farah.

Emma was convicted of murder and sentenced as a juvenile to be detained at Her Majesty's pleasure, despite evidence that she had been subjected to extreme violence during the course of their six-month relationship.

Now she is hoping to get the murder conviction overturned, with the support of campaigners nationwide.

At the original court hearing 10 years ago there was evidence that

Emma was beaten, sexually assaulted and prevented from leaving the house because Trevor had nailed down the windows and locked the telephone in his car.

On the night that Emma killed him, she was said to be in a complete state of terror. She said he was about to rape her and she feared he might kill her.

Now Emma is pinning her hopes on an appeal hearing on 26 June at the Court of Appeal, in London, in front of Lord Chief Justice Taylor.

Her case was taken up by feminist campaigning organisation Justice for Women. Emma contacted them in 1992 after another woman, Kiranjit Ahluwalia, who was jailed for killing her husband, had her murder conviction quashed and was released from jail.

Said a spokeswoman for Justice for

Women: "It was when Kiranjit's murder conviction was quashed and she was released from prison that Emma realised her case was also a miscarriage of justice.

"She has already spent over 10 years in Holloway prison, in London, longer than many of the periods served by premeditated murderers."

The campaign to free Emma has won the support of thousands of people, including many MPs, Lords, celebrities and individuals. Supporters include actress Julie Christie, MP Glenda Jackson, and Ceredigion MP Cynog Dafis.

"As a result of the growing campaign to free Emma, the case was now recognised that her abandonment of her right to appeal eight years ago was as a result of the lasting effect of severe trauma," added the spokeswoman for Justice for Women, which can be contacted at 55 Rathcoole Gardens, London N8 9NE.

■ Emma Humphreys

Belated appeal for woman who killed violent lover

Duncan Campbell reports on what women's groups claim is a classic defence case of provocation

A WOMAN convicted of the murder of her violent lover will finally have her appeal heard next week — 10 years after she was jailed for life. The case is seen by lawyers and women's groups as a classic example of one in which the defence of provocation is justified.

Emma Humphreys, aged 27, who was born in Dolgellau in Wales, was jailed for life at Nottingham crown court in 1985 for the murder of Trevor Armitage. She met him and began living with him when she was working as a prostitute in Nottingham." I was a mixed-up 16-year-old and he was a mixed-up 33-year-old," she says.

Mr Armitage, who had one conviction for assaulting a prostitute and another for grievous bodily harm against a taxi driver, became increasingly jealous of her and demanded to know how much she earned and what she did with her clients. She says he regularly raped her when she refused to sleep with him.

On February 25, 1985, she went with a taxi-driver to have a drink to get change for her fare. Mr Armitage saw her and was angry that she was with another man. She says she realised that he would be angry with her that night and, slashed her wrists, something she had done many times before, thinking that this would divert his anger.

Ms Humphreys says that she believed that she was about to be attacked, shot her eyes and stabbed him once.

Now in Holloway prison, north London, where she has been for the past ten and a half years, she says she hopes that finally her case will be heard. She signed an abandonment of her appeal eight years ago because she was unaware that there were any grounds for appeal on the grounds of long-term provocation.

The abandonment was nullified at the Court of Appeal last January. On Thursday, the full appeal will be heard by Lord Justice Taylor and two other

judges. It is seen as a key case in the issue of battered women killing partners.

"I have never been to the Court of Appeal before so I don't know what to expect," said Ms Humphreys. She said she had had a visit from Kiranjit Ahluwalia, who was freed from a life sentence for the murder of her violent husband in 1992 and who had told her what to expect in court.

If successful, she hopes to enter a small residential home where people receive counselling for two years.

"I've had a lot of support from people now but as a way it's all 20 years too late," she said, fingering an African good-luck charm that hangs round her neck.

As a child she was attacked by her alcoholic step-father and became a runaway and prostitute at 13, working as such in Canada, where her mother now lives, and in Nottingham, where her father lives.

Although she would almost certainly have been released on

parole by now — the tariff for her sentence was originally set at six years and then raised to eight by the Home Secretary — if she had not embarked on the appeal, she is adamant that she wants the murder verdict quashed. She would plead guilty to manslaughter on grounds of provocation.

Inside prison she spends most of her time writing poetry. One poem, which she had intended to send to the appeal judges, recounts how she cut her wrists for the first time in the school gym when she was 12.

Harriet Wistrich, of Justice for Women, said: "Domestic violence is still often not seen as sufficient provocation for women like Emma Humphreys.

"...Emma has spent a great deal longer in prison than many men who have killed women known to them."

In 1994, 101 men killed women known to them. Of those, 29 per cent were convicted of murder in the same year, 13 women killed men known to them and 40 per cent were convicted of murder. An estimated 76 women are currently in prison for killing their violent husbands.

Emma Humphreys: abandoned appeal eight years ago because she was unaware that she had any grounds of provocation

rather than a honky-tonk angel. She was sentenced to be detained at Her Majesty's pleasure.

Taken to Durham jail, the cut her wrists on a regular basis, although she says she does not have the guts to kill herself, and spent a lot of time in the strip cells. She was moved to Holloway and has taken a course in journalism. Following the case of Kiranjit Ahluwalia, the Indian woman jailed for killing her violent husband but freed after a retrial when the extent of her husband's violence became known, she decided to do something about her case.

She contacted Anna Reynolds when she had met in Durham jail before she was cleared on appeal and who now runs the prison magazine Inside Time. Reynolds put her in touch with Justice for Women, which has taken up the cases of women who had killed violent men and which has campaigned for the release of Sara Thornton, serving life for killing her husband.

Julie Bindel, of Justice for Women, says that "because Emma was sentenced as a juvenile, there was no tariff on her life sentence. For this reason there is no idea of how long she could serve."

The Thornton and Ahluwalia cases have brought the widest coverage to the issue of women who kill violent husbands and their separa

Part 2

The Struggle for Justice

Emma being interviewed by BBC Nottingham, spring 1993.

3: Justice for Women

Emma Humphreys had never contemplated an appeal; in fact, shortly after her conviction, she bizarrely and under the gaze of her then legal team signed an abandonment of appeal, thus waiving all of her rights.

Sentenced as a juvenile to be to be detained 'At Her Majesty's pleasure', Emma had spent ten years in prison, knowing that she had suffered an injustice, and yet without any faith in being able to receive fair treatment from the legal process. This chapter describes the campaign that led to her freedom, the relationships and the components of professionalism, support and friendship for a woman who dared to accommodate her guilt for taking a person's life with the injustice of being labelled a murderer.

Emma's condition following Armitage's death, and the life which had led up to that night – her feelings of remorse, bereavement and confusion – should by any standards have suggested an environment where she would be carefully contained; debriefed by someone skilled in understanding the effects of both acute and chronic trauma; given physical and medical care; fed with nourishing and non-toxic food and medication; and gradually surrounded by a therapeutic intervention. There she could have addressed and confronted what had happened to Armitage, and could have engaged in her own history and how she had come to be where she was in her life.

This was a young woman whose earliest memory was of her father smashing open her mother's nose, and her mother taking a knife to him. Her later childhood memories were of her mother abusing alcohol and being beaten by her stepfather. Her last memory in freedom was of taking a knife to a man who was violent and abusive towards her. Whatever processes, psychological and emotional, that led her to complete that circle, were inevitably to be locked up within her with the murder conviction. Whatever this teenager *needed*, what she *got* was prison: Durham prison.

However, Emma's distress and deprivation was such that prison was a kind of refuge for her. A women's space, where at least she would not be abused by men. It was a place where she could experience security and kindness, in an environment where, according to home office research, 75% of the inmates suffered psychological distress and mental health problems. She wrote to Julie Bindel: "I've never met women like I came across in my house at Drake – it was actually hell." However, she also found some safe relationships, forming friendships and relationships with other troubled women, sometimes believing that they would live in sanctuary together forever. Sharp lessons were learned as Emma herself and her friends and lovers were moved from one prison to another with sometimes just a few hours notice, sometimes never to be seen again for years.

Emma was moved from the Victorian Durham to Styal – where in the eighties, probation and education services attempted to offer radical education and self-development programs to women – on to Drake Hall, and then to the newly renovated Holloway. But through this Emma's anorexia, which she says began before she was eight years old, was not picked up or treated. Before she was imprisoned, her self-medication of choice was alcohol; in fact, Emma described herself as becoming an alcoholic as the relationship with Trevor deteriorated. However, her asylum did not herald a treatment programme, a detoxification. Instead it offered her new soothers: prescription medication, cannabis, amphetamines, barbiturates, heroin. She said that anything and everything was available, to be picked up at will. Her incarceration substituted an addiction to alcohol with an addiction to prescription medication.

Emma started to pick up on her education in prison, signing

up for every course available, beginning to write and attend creative writing classes, and eventually winning the Koestler prize for writing. Like many women whose physical and emotional integrity have been compromised by chronic violence, she explored and confronted her self and her humanity in her writings, and gained a sense of herself as a person who was worthy of respect and as a woman who could be political. Her poem, 'Borderline', not only invites the reader into her own experience, but lays down a delicious challenge to the psychiatric profession which blithely diagnoses women such as Emma, living with the legacy of violence on their mental health, as having 'borderline personality disorder'.

Justice for Women, and later the court, were convinced by Emma's own story that she had the right to an appeal – told, as she said, after only a couple of years of eventually talking to people about her life and her offence; written without any justification; and simply recounting "what happened". But she had signed that right away. Even if Justice for Women succeeded in getting an appeal, there were obstacles to winning: on her arrest Emma, under the supervision of a duty solicitor, had allowed the police to construct a statement which propelled her inevitably towards a conviction for murder. She had said little, and had waited for the inevitable sentence. So in the legal papers of the time there was little to help Emma, and much to damn her. She spoke of Armitage as her boyfriend; she did not talk about her history and the history of their relationship.

At that time the current law measured the actions of an alleged murderer against the extent to which a 'reasonable man' would be provoked. The problem with this was that Emma was a woman, with different experiences from the legal notion of a reasonable man. This was not a fight between two men of equal weight and reason in the street. This was a woman who was already vulnerable when she entered the relationship with Armitage, a relationship during which she was sexually and physically abused. Yet in the statement, Emma had said that she had meant to kill him, and agreed that it was because Trevor had taunted her about cutting her wrists. She said that the police and the solicitor had kept saying that "Trevor wasn't any good anyway", trying to make her defend herself. But Emma said that she did not want to hear that, she thought that she loved him, and that she had done a terrible thing in killing him.

The law could not begin to comprehend a vulnerable woman, chronically abused by men, and with the effects of cumulative provocation by this man. Neither could it comprehend that, because of Emma's vulnerable state, she essentially became the chief witness in her prosecution. Thus manslaughter on the grounds of provocation was denied, and she was convicted of murder and sentenced to serve the devastating 'at Her Majesty's pleasure': "They interrogated me as an adult, tried me as an adult and sentenced me as a juvenile."

When she wrote her first letter to Justice for Women in 1992, Emma would not have considered herself a feminist. During the feminist activism of the seventies she was a troubled child, and prison had cauterised any connection or involvement in theory or activism. But what she did have was years of experience of living with her own and other women's issues, not least of male violence and oppression. She was writing to a campaign with a history of which she was unaware, but that could not have been in a better position to grasp the core issue on which her injustice was based.

Among the Women's Liberation Movement's political innovations was its investigation of personal oppression. Working from the mantra 'the personal is political', the movement created sanctuary for women who needed to flee from danger in their own home: refuges which mushroomed throughout the country, and later throughout the world. Battered women's refuges effected a revolution in consciousness about the motives and meanings of violence in intimate relationships between men and women. By providing a safe and supportive space for women on the run from a violent partner who were bereft of resources – except themselves – property and protection, by helping women to make sense of what they'd endured, and to make a plan for their future, an archive of evidence about domestic violence had emerged.

Domestic violence was exposed as something that revealed men's dominion over women. Domestic violence, therefore, exemplified defining themes of contemporary feminism: the revelation of violence as a *resource* for masculinity; and the importance of self-esteem and empowerment for women for whom oppression inhabited every nook and cranny of their existence. Battered women's lives exemplified the matrix where economic and psychic resources met: lives starved of economic autonomy, self-respect, and freedom of movement; lives in which survival demanded great vigilance in the face of overwhelming force.

Refuges were created across Britain in the late seventies, based on a culture of women's liberation committed to self-discovery, recovery from oppression, and self-determination. Those networks had a profound impact on public service and policing – they simultaneously challenged and changed public services, from housing to policing, which had failed to appreciate the dangerousness of domestic violence, and domestic violence as a dramatisation of the problem of patriarchy in contemporary Britain.

By the eighties, refuges for battered women, run by the women's movement, had become a more or less permanent auxiliary to municipal services. That was the decade when feminism's impact became increasingly institutionalised: in the academy; and in municipalities that adopted equal opportunities programmes and anti-oppression intiatives.

Consciousness about sexual violence was also amplified by cases that triggered public outrage, fear and sympathy. The treatment of two young women, the Maw sisters in Yorkshire, who killed their father after a lifetime of sadistic and sexual abuse perpetrated against the girls and their mother, provoked outrage. The way that the police reacted to the serial murders by the 'Yorkshire Ripper' – from their representation of the victims as 'respectable' women or 'prostitutes'; to their virtual curfew on women in Yorkshire during their investigation; to their failure to respect the accounts of survivors who were able to offer descriptions of the killer – exposed the sexism that motivated the murders, but that also penetrated, and often paralysed, police investigations. Public opinion was also stunned by documentary-maker Roger Graef's fly-on-the-wall television film about Thames Valley police investigations into rape cases, in which a woman was treated as if she were a suspect whose story deserved only to be challenged. All of these cases, and more, prompted protests and debates that resonated with a fatalistic fear of men, and faded discourses about masculinity as dangerousness. Undoubtedly they resonated with the new awareness that feminism ignited.

During the 1970s the Women's Liberation Movement added violence against women to its short schedule of basic demands. But feminism itself was engaged in tough and enduring debates about the meanings of violence and masculinity, often framed within the formative polarisation between radical feminism and socialist feminism. This was one of several critical cleavages within women's liberation that increasingly rendered the 1970s' form of women's liberation – a movement anchored in the theatre of campaigning and in the notion of sisterhood – unsustainable. Cleavages over the concept of 'woman', and over differences between women derived from class, ethnicity and sexual orientation, disturbed the ethic of sisterhood as an open and unifying political practice.

The polarisation between 'radical feminism' and 'socialist feminism' did not exhaust the many possible tendencies within the movement, but defined a significant part of its internal debate. Those differences were re-visited by the emergence of 'masculinity' as a feminist problematic, the salience of patriarchy as a unifying concept in feminist politics, and of sexual identities and subjectivities. Cleavages persisted into the 1980s, a decade in which feminism began to find an institutional expression. Though that produced fresh paradoxes: some activists felt that the new decade was less flexible and less inventive than in the 1970s, when women were improving new political forms and themes.

The successful spread of feminist concerns into traditional structures presented new difficulties: for an anti-hierarchical movement, the expansion of some of its self-help systems into services with paid workers inaugurated power differentials that its culture was ill-equipped to settle. In the 1980s the adoption of some feminist concerns in some local authorities, particularly in London, undoubtedly marked a new relationship between the local state and one of the most resonant social movements of its time. It was also the decade when new social movements concerned with racism, disability and ecology joined older social movements among urban residents, and found a palpable presence in the local state. But the dialogue between the women's movement and local government was not without difficulty: ideas and services associated with an informal movement, dedicated to an anti-hierarchical culture and generic skills, were entering a civil service culture based on diverse professional disciplines, stiff hierarchies, and systems of accountability and representivity.

Unsurprisingly, says Professor Liz Kelly, director of the Child and Woman Abuse Studies Unit, London Metropolitan University, the ideological transmission was often imperfect. But the women's movement was also confronting new contradictions in its own practice: it was increasingly difficult, she felt, to sustain the combination of "service provision to extremely needy and damaged women with political engagement in sexual politics". Some feminists felt alienated from town hall politics: from the 'identity politics' which had been vital in the excavation of the contours of difference between women, and which for some women attracted anxiety; or from the institutionalisation or professionalisation of feminist concerns; from reactive campaigning prompted by some outrage or other.

The judicial landscape was littered with the bodies of women and children murdered by men, whose deaths were slowly but surely provoking a new awareness about dangerousness. In the child protection professions, inquiries into child deaths began to have a dramatic impact on statutory services. There was no parallel response to the deaths of women killed by their partners, but the network of refuges had alerted activists and some professionals to the scale of, and secrecy surrounding, domestic violence. And feminists in the criminal justice system were beginning to make connections between domestic violence and the narratives of women serving life sentences for killing their partners. In New York State's Bedford Hill prison, run by a feminist governor, a hearing had been organised enabling women serving life sentences for murder to tell their story to an assembly of professionals, politicians and judges.

In Britain, the case of Kiranjit Ahluwalia exposed the magnetic power of shame and honour, familialism and ostracism; the failure of statutory services to bring vigilance to victimised Black women; and finally the threshold that she crossed when she set alight to her sleeping assailant. Her case attracted an unprecedented coalition between professionals and activists, between Black and white women, that inaugurated a new awareness of homicide and gender.

Kiranjit Ahluwalia was an Asian woman who had been forced to abandon her law studies and marry Deepak Ahluwalia when she was 23 years old. Instantly the marriage was dominated by his determination to control her life. For a decade she endured rape and violence. She was treated like a slave. His regime of terror shrouded her two children, too. Finally, in 1989, feeling that she could neither escape nor endure any more, she set fire to his bedclothes. She had not intended to kill him, but ten days later Deepak Ahluwalia died of his injuries. Kiranjit was tried for murder. The trial judge deemed her history of violence "not serious". The prosecution described it merely as being "knocked about". Her plea of manslaughter due to provocation was rejected by the jury. She was convicted of murder.

A white women's group in Crawley were so concerned about her story that they contacted Britain's most vigorous Black feminist group, Southall Black Sisters, to campaign on her behalf. SBS was a campaigning group in West London, formed in 1979, that provided direct services to women, and also organised campaigns to address racism as well as sexism within Black communities. SBS had experienced considerable hostility within the community for helping women to escape domestic violence, but, according to Hannana Siddiqui, "it was the campaign for Kiranjit Ahluwalia that changed things within the community."

Usually SBS had responded to the deaths of women, but this case introduced a new dimension: a woman's agency and the context of despair and consequences of desperate measures.

What these groups had to confront was the problem of time: the time between Deepak Ahluwalia's last attack, his falling asleep, and Kiranjit's action. The argument between the prosecution and defence illuminated the different interpretations brought to men's and women's resources and options. Were those hours to be deemed – as they were debated in the trial – a 'cooling down' period or a 'boiling over' period? How was provocation to be understood? Did it relate to an instant reaction, one protagonist confronting the other, mobilising a 'reasonable' response to attack? But how were the unequal powers of a man and a woman to be understood through their strategies? At her trial, Kiranjit's plea of manslaughter due to provocation was rejected by the jury, and she was found guilty of murder.

Kiranjit Ahluwalia's case attracted national attention, not least because of the woman herself: a woman whose family life until her marriage had been stable and fond; a woman who had not been ruined by life; whose modest eloquence (though she could speak little English) amplified the sense that her husband's violence and her trial were grave injustices. It also created an embryonic alliance to challenge the homicide laws. Two national women's organisations, the Women's Institute and the Townswomen's Guild, often assumed to be conservative, enlisted in support of women who killed their violent partners. The Townswomen's Guild was to produce a poster highlighting the sexist interpretation of provocation: "Man strangles nagging wife . . . sentence 18 months suspended"; "after years of violent abuse, woman stabs husband . . . sentence life." A Guild petition attracted 40,000 signatures.

Towards the end of the 1980s, many feminists were thinking afresh about how to express their politics and campaigns. Justice for Women's impetus came, then, from activists with a long history of campaigning against violence against women, and from that alliance with SBS. "We joined up with Justice for Women on the homicide laws – I suspect it has been one of our closest campaigns with white women," says Hannana Saddiqui. "Kiranjit's case galvanised women, it was revelatory, it changed consciousness about the homicide laws and domestic violence. We didn't expect that to happen. It was major."

The Ahluwalia case dramatised both the cruelty endured by women and children in families and the sexism of the criminal justice system. But the double injustice of an unendurable life saturated with violence, and the drastically different response to women and men, drew attention to the way that men and women's troubles, pre-occupations and identities were invoked: men killing women, their honour affronted, citing provocation by treacherous, hectoring, lascivious and unreasonable women, receiving light sentences; women killing men and receiving life sentences, their histories routinely interred, unaddressed by a system that was simultaneously uninterested and foxed by these women. Julie Bindel remembered the case as a paradox: "It was steeped in cultural idiosyncracies, and yet generic." Hannana Saddiqui believes that it ultimately "challenged the way that people thought about miscarriages of justice". This appeal raised awareness nationally, and was significant in bringing feminist activism into the mainstream gaze and understanding.

In 1992 Kiranjit was granted an appeal on the grounds that her original trial had not heard evidence she was suffering from a form of depression at the time of the offence which may have given rise to the defence of diminished responsibility. The court of appeal rejected the argument that provocation should also have been available as a defence, because of the time span between the last act of abuse and the killing. Importantly, however, the Lord Chief Justice at the time, who delivered judgment, did rule that the gap between the last act of provocation and the killing did not have to be immediate, provided that the loss of self-control was 'sudden and temporary'. This was an important acknowledgement of the feminist argument that women in a domestic violence context may react more slowly than a man to an act of provocation. At her re-trial, Kiranjit was offered the opportunity by the Crown to plead guilty to manslaughter on the grounds of diminished responsibility.

Ahluwalia's case had earlier been featured in a Dispatches documentary for Channel 4 television, 'The Provoked Wife', made by Gita Saghal of Southall Black Sisters. The programme also featured the cases of other women serving life sentences for killing their violent partners, including Sara Thornton and Amelia Rossiter. Meanwhile Sara Thornton's case had been taken up by West Yorkshire Justice for Women, who during the eighties had supported the Maw sisters convicted of manslaughter after killing their abusive father. Sandra McNeill said that the Justice for Women campaign in Leeds was inspired by Southall Black Sisters. Women with long histories of activism in Leeds also knew that they had to change their approach. Campaigning for individual women was not enough; they had to change the law. In the early nineties this group, whilst demonstrating, postering and picketing, also prepared carefully argued papers for the Royal Commission on Criminal Justice, and targeted politicians who they felt could influence this process.

A cluster of cases constituted a kind of political critical mass. Janet Gardner was a woman who had ended her relationship with Peter Iles after nine months because of his sadistic behaviour – he beat her, burned her with cigarettes, pinned her to a chair and cut her with a knife, and once he tried to cut her throat. She had tried everything to escape: changing her address; her telephone number; calling the police; seeking injunctions. He trailed and tormented her for four years, and finally during one attack she grabbed a knife and stabbed him. She believed then that: "If I hadn't done what I did, he'd have killed me." Gardner's case was taken up by the newly formed coalition of Justice for Women and Southall Black Sisters. She had been convicted of manslaughter, but sentenced to five years imprisonment. At an appeal against sentence her sentence, shortly after the Ahluwalia case, her sentence was cut to one year.

Sara Thornton's husband Malcolm Thornton, an alcoholic former police officer, had been consistently violent to Sara and made threats to her ten-year-old daughter throughout their 18-month relationship. Already on a charge of assault on the night that he died, he threatened to kill Sara while she slept. Fearing for her life, she went to look for his truncheon, pleaded for him to go to bed, and when he refused, picked up a knife and stabbed him once. Sara Thornton's defence team put forward a plea of guilty to manslaughter on the grounds of diminished responsibility, but completely ignored the issue of the cumulative effects of abuse. Judge and jury rejected the plea, and she was convicted of murder.

In Thornton's first Appeal in 1991 she put forward a defence of provocation, which was rejected by the judges because the sixty seconds which it took to get a knife undermined her defence of 'sudden and temporary loss of control'. The judge stated that Sara could have "walked out or gone upstairs". However, at the appeal it had been argued that women subjected to domestic violence might not react immediately, and the concept of 'slow burn provocation' was born. Sandra McNeill of West Yorkshire Justice for Women explained that the issue on which Kiranjit's provocation defence caused difficulty was present in the Thornton Appeal: the time that had elapsed between the last act of abuse and the time of the killing – even though in Thornton's case it was reduced to sixty seconds.

Two days after the Thornton result, Joseph Mcgrail, who had killed his partner Marion Kennedy by kicking her in the stomach when she was drunk, had his plea of manslaughter on the grounds of provocation accepted by a sympathetic judge who said that: "this woman would have tried the patience of a saint." Mcgrail walked free without a trial. This galvanised the Justice for Women campaign to focus on a law which allowed men to get away with murder by fielding a defence which focused on the histories of their women victims, whilst women were suffering miscarriages of justice because the abusive histories of their male perpetrators were being erased.Following the failure of Sara Thornton's first appeal, Justice for Women's campaign regrouped and immediately started to lobby to convince the Home secretary that her case warranted another appeal.

Julie Bindel went to see Mike O'Brien, the newly-elected Labour MP for Atherstone (Sara Thornton's constituency), to secure his support. O'Brien felt that Thornton was not the best case to run: it was complicated. Justice for Women's reaction was: "Whoa! We've never been bothered about that", and they carried on with the campaign. The campaign was not concerned with the difficulties or the complexities of cases, but the justice of them. When the Thornton appeal was to be heard, the Leeds group asked friends and activists in London to organise the demonstration. Julie Bindel and Harriet Wistrich had been involved with a campaign to support a Hassidic woman who had been shunned by her Hackney community for trying to protect her children from abuse, and had a framework for organising a campaign already. This alliance between West Yorkshire and London on the Thornton appeal gave birth to Justice for Women, and set the template for a campaign which would be forensic, energetic, and, always, witty.

They joined with the November women's action group and organised a huge march through central London, focussing on the injustices of 'battered women who kill'. Southall Black Sisters supported the campaign and lent their experience, although the media mostly called Justice for Women rather than SBS, despite the long history of SBS campaigning and expertise. There was a general perception that SBS only dealt with 'Black women's issues'.

Justice for Women was finally formed as a campaign. The experience of these cases encouraged the activists to be more than a support group for a woman trying to appeal: to become a campaign group. This became a feminist campaign like no other, the first truly modern campaign which insisted on mainstreaming the issues and going to the heart of the Establishment; an establishment which had been responsible for sustaining the patriarchy under which these women had suffered, and which could not provide the tools to give them a fair trial. MPs, Judges and lawyers were approached. Harriet Wistrich said that they made a point of making friends with journalists, and watching, listening and learning fast how to campaign in the modern world.

They produced briefing papers, with background information

and suggested storylines and angles on other issues of the day. They put up media spokespeople, they produced soundbites – "men getting away with murder", "the nagging and shagging defence" – which resonated in the public mind. They appeared on television programmes, thoroughly briefed, looking good, able to engage on the screen with anyone – whether a man or a Tory – and to give a serious and sparky account of themselves. They produced posters and teeshirts. Whatever the news story, if they could connect it, however tangentially, to the campaign to change the law in relation to battered women who kill, they would appear and give an opinion. Journalists were given access to women prisoners and to victims of male violence and prostitution, supported by press packs . This small, determinedly non-organisation ran campaigns as if it were a corporate lobbyist. One journalist told Harriet Wistrich at the time that the Emma Humphreys press pack was one of the best that they had ever seen.

Duncan Campbell was one of the journalists who reported these cases for the Guardian. "Justice for Women and Southall Black Sisters were great, very proactive, very helpful about providing access, very undefensive. I dealt with Julie Bindel, she was always very straightforward and good fun to work with. They made a point of letting the women involved speak for themselves, arranging prison visits and trusting the journalist concerned rather than invigilating the in-prison interviews. I was a great fan of theirs and trusted their judgement."

In May 1994 Harry Cohen tried to introduce a Bill to amend the 1957 Homicide Act, and drew attention to the highly gendered bias of the law on provocation: "The injustice that I seek to remove is the blatantly sexist application of the law in homicide cases and the availability of the plea of provocation. At the heart of the matter is the law that specifies that the conviction of murder carries a mandatory life sentence. It is despicable that a woman who has suffered years of sustained domestic violence and acts out of fear and desperation on behalf of herself or her children should be treated as a common murderer and put away for life . . . it has been obvious for years that the law operates two different systems when deciding what is provocation for men and what is provocation for women. Women are always barred from pleading provocation if the death was not the result of an immediate and 'sudden loss of control'."

The deal with both Sara Thornton and Emma Humphreys was clear and overt. Justice for Women would campaign for them if the women would join the campaign and work for other women. However, this was not uncomplicated. Harriet Wistrich and Julie Bindel said that they had long discussions amongst their colleagues about the implications, the difficulties, and the ethics. Once a woman began to take her space in the media, she could be transformed into a signifier, an icon, for other campaigns, other women, other issues.

The celebrity that was 'Emma' brought its own strains, not least because she began to encounter real difficulties with prison officials, who resurrected a previously dormant standing order for prisoners not to speak to the media after her press and television appearances began to engage public sympathy. Emma's letters to Julie and Harriet, and the letter to Governor King, describe the room searches, the cancelled leave and the juxtaposition of her powerlessness and lack of agency as a prisoner, just at the time when through her public storytelling she was becoming personally empowered. Nevertheless, Emma continued with her public campaign, believing that this was the most effective way for the injustice of her own case and that of other women to become understood.

Sandra McNeill said that not all women were able to fight publicly, and the campaign realised that it was important to have a strategy which did not identify the women if individual circumstances made that more appropriate. For example, the Wakefield mother who killed a man after he had raped a member of her family could not be publicised in the same way, because of the effects on her children.

Justice for Women released the campaigning imperative: "It was a group of women, all of whom had activist histories, and some of whom were involved in direct service provision," says

Liz Kelly, "but whose feminist interest was in a feminist campaigning voice in the public sphere, and who wanted to focus their energy on that. What was important to me about Justice for Women was that it was not about direct service provision, though it did involve providing day-to-day support to some women. And it did not go down the route of employing paid workers."

Julie Bindel remembers the day that Emma Humphreys' letter arrived – she was due to be at a meeting that Saturday afternoon, and although the campaign often received letters from prison, this was different. "It was the eloquence! It was beautifully written, and you felt 'oh, poor thing.' She was so young, she'd written to so many people, including the miscarriages of justice campaign, Rough Justice, who had suggested that she write instead to Justice for Women. We thought we had to do something. It could not have been a more straightforward case. We wrote to see her in prison, and we told her that an appeal would keep her in prison because she would not be able to go on with the parole process. She said: 'So what, I don't want to come out a murderer!' "

When Julie visited Emma in Holloway "she was quite stroppy, very vulnerable, she had scars all the way up her arms. She had an attitude: pissed off! And she was very sweet and vulnerable, and grateful that I'd gone to see her. She was wearing a very tight, tarty top, which showed how thin she was. She had long hair, blow-dried, nail varnish. She looked like she was in clink – she had the smell of prison. I told her about Justice for Women and – I was trying to make her laugh – that we weren't middle class missionaries out to save her. I explained what we wanted to do: change the law. And we were looking for cases that could challenge the law. I also explained that we would not be a support group, but that we would take up her case, and that the only way to do it was to use publicity. I asked if she was up for that?"

"She was just rotting in there, she was angry. She had felt that she was being punished, rightly, for what she'd done, and it was Kiranjit's case that made her think. She'd massively minimised what had happened to her, and that's why it was so important to tell her *entire* story. We understood that there was no way we'd get anywhere by focusing only on her relationship with

Trevor Armitage. It was more complicated than that: she was already a vulnerable person who became even more vulnerable in her relationship with him." Since arriving in prison, Emma had been on medication. It was then controlled, she only had a "slight slur, but she was not zonked. She was probably using illegal drugs, too, she could get her hands on anything. She knew the currency."

After Julie reported back to the campaign that this woman had no legal representation, it was decided to ask Rohit Sanghvi, who had acted for Kiranjit Ahluwalia, Janet Gardner, and Sara Thornton in her first appeal, to take on her case. As no legal aid was available, Rohit said that he would need the help of someone from the group to take a detailed background statement. Harriet Wistrich, a film-maker training to be a lawyer, volunteered to take the statement that would be the biography, something which took many hours of painstaking work over months for both her and Emma in Holloway prison. During that time, the relationship which had started out as being between lawyer/campaigner and prisoner developed into something more engaged: friend and supporter.

Rohit was keen for Emma's case to be led by the same barrister, Edward Fitzgerald, who had acted for Janet Gardner. But Justice for Women were by now determined that it was important to field women as Emma's advocates. Vera Baird was an experienced, progressive barrister who had applied for silk. She was well-known as a top criminal barrister, and also for her triumphant defence of miners charged with riot after the battle of Orgeave during the marathon miners strike in 1984-5. Vera started afresh on Emma's case: "She was very little, very young, very fragile, perceptive but uneducated – it screamed out that she only did what she did because she faced overwhelming forces. I told her, 'give us a while, we'll do what we can to launch an appeal.' When we came out of Holloway prison, after our first meeting with Emma, Harriet asked, 'what grounds?' I said 'we'll find something'."

Vera thought it unlikely that 'murder' described the killing of Trevor Armitage: there had to be an intention to murder. It seemed likely that diminished responsibility or provocation could be invoked. However, before the grounds of appeal could be considered, there were two huge legal hurdles to overcome. Shortly after her conviction, Emma had signed an 'abandonment' of her right to appeal. In order to proceed with an appeal now, it was necessary to 'nullify' the abandonment, by showing that Emma had not appreciated the significance of what she had signed. Second, an appeal needed to be lodged within 28 days; therefore an application for leave to appeal ten years out of time had to be made.

Vera discovered that the counsel who had defended Emma during her trial was now a judge. He had been competent, but had been working at a time when there was little appreciation in the courts of the impact of men's violence against women. When he was contacted he readily accepted that, though he'd done his best, he'd never felt he had succeeded in communicating with her properly. Vera felt that was the key – Emma had not understood the conditions in which a defendant may appeal. When her barrister went to see her in her cell after she'd been convicted of murder, she would have been in such a state of shock he felt no confidence that she would have understood the necessary next steps.

Although an appeal had been sent to an Appeal Court judge and rejected, it had not been followed up by an application to the full court. But the failure to follow up was a problem for the lawyers. Vera Baird reckoned it was "nothing to the problems it caused Emma". At a key moment Emma had been summonsed to the prison's legal advice officer, together with another prisoner, to receive the news of the judge's decision. Vera recalls: "They agreed they'll do their sentences together. Emma is called in, told the bad news and invited to sign a paper giving up future rights to appeal. That document was the problem." The only way forward was to show that she had not understood what she was doing. "This case really shows how this document – inviting you to renounce your rights forever – should not be offered to prisoners. It is a wicked thing to ask someone to do. Prisoners are in a state of shock, and how can they know what will emerge? It's a wicked document. We tried to find a way round it."

The application for leave to appeal was based upon Emma's biography, and on the view that she had not understood the implications of what she'd done after her conviction. The court was reluctant: surely everything had been explained to her at the time? Vera bargained: if the original barrister was convinced that Emma had understood that she was signing away her right to appeal, so be it, but if not, then clearly that would support her case, she argued. The court agreed to hear what the barrister had to say. In fact, both the barrister and his junior at the trial wrote affidavits saying that they doubted whether she'd understood. Her solicitor, too, had never felt that he'd effectively communicated with her. When Vera Baird submitted Emma's social service files and these affidavits, the court agreed. "We were given leave to appeal out of time. It was almost unique." So important was the decision that the Court of Appeal suggested a second counsel should be appointed to lead the case.

Justice for Women enlisted an eminent barrister, Helen Grindrod, with a strong reputation as both a defender and prosecutor – in a prescient case she had prosecuted British Nuclear Fuels for leaking radioactive waste – and, like Baird, a feminist, a socialist active among progressive lawyers. They believed that Helen's own background, her familiarity with working class life, her commitment to women, and her politics would illuminate this case.

By the mid-1990s they were familiar with the notion of 'battered women's syndrome' and 'learned helplessness' fielded in the American courts, and they were sceptical. In any case, it could not help explain the catastrophic events the night Trevor Armitage died: this had only been a short relationship; Emma had been out working as a prostitute; she then joined Armitage and others in a pub, and Armitage began talking about the pleasures of a gang bang. She believed he meant her. A short while before there had been a violent confrontation between them – after he'd abused her, she'd broken into his house and smashed his windows, for which she'd received a short prison sentence. Although this was a relatively short relationship there was already a pattern: he was violent. If he wanted sex it had to happen; if she didn't want it then he raped her.

But the genesis of the provocation law was rooted in a very different circumstance: it was enacted in the 1957 Homicide Act to mitigate capital punishment for patriarchy. The law was concerned with a man convicted of murder after arriving at his home to find his woman with another man. It was constructed around conventions of what a reasonable man might be expected to tolerate. "So, a reasonable person was always a man," comments Vera Baird. "And the court had muddled up the concept of a reasonable person with a person who behaved rationally." Over time, however, the limits of that narrow definition were being challenged.

Kiranjit Ahluwalia's re-trial had also yielded an important recognition that the law on provocation did not require the behaviour to have happened immediately before the killing, merely the 'loss of control'. "That opened the door to saying that provocation could go a long way back. We stepped into that space," says Vera Baird. The significance of this was that it allowed the woman's history, and its consequences on her well-being, to be brought to bear upon her action.

Another case proved to be helpful to Baird and Grindrod. Two brothers had killed their father after many years of abuse. One brother had left home; the other remained, and continued to suffer. The killing occurred when the first brother returned and the father resumed the abuse. Together, they killed him. The first brother was convicted of murder, the second of manslaughter. The reasoning had been that only the second brother could claim the provocation defence. In the appeal the barrister, John Kay, argued that not only had the first brother also been abused by the father upon his return, but that his motivation was also animated by the knowledge of what had been happening to his brother. The Court of Appeal concluded that it had been wrong to dismiss the impact of historic abuse.

The lawyers also addressed the issue of loss of control: Emma Humphreys had an explosive emotional history, a traumatic and neglectful childhood, followed by institutionalisation, depression and self harm. To ask how any 'reasonable man' might act would not help understand her reactions. What needed to be addressed was how this woman, with this history, living with these forces ranged against her, might act. Trevor Armitage had not created the difficulties and dangers in Emma's life, but his abusive behaviour was the last straw in a short life shaped by neglect and peopled by dangerous men.

At Emma's trial, it appeared that the ignition to her fatal action had been contained in two things: the deceased approaching Emma without wearing trousers; and his mockery of her for failing to successfully commit suicide. The question was: did she lose control because of his behaviour? But the lawyers discovered that there had been cases in which provocation did not need to be so confined, it could be anything that contributed to the event.

When Emma's case came before the Appeal Court in June 1995, it was vital for the lawyers to establish the criteria by which the Appeal Court could consider the relevant characteristic of provocation in her case. The Crown relied on a narrow definition of a reasonable person, "but the argument that no reasonable person would slash their wrists was just forlorn," recalls Vera Baird.

With a large and optimistic feminist crowd outside the Appeal Court and the tiny figure of Emma Humphreys inside, Baird and Grindrod persuaded the Appeal Court to take seriously their two key points: timing; and what constituted a rational reaction. The campaigners knew that they'd won: the court would grant the appeal. They'd changed the law: what now had to be taken into account in future cases was anything that had been said or done that could contribute to 'loss of control'; the last provocation could not be separated from its pre-history, including far back into childhood experience.

Unexpectedly, they had to wait a week for the judgment, during which time Emma returned to prison. On 7 July 1995 the judgment was delivered to a packed courtroom: Emma's conviction for murder was overturned. The judges suggested that she might want to slip out of the back entrance, away from the cameras. But no, she wanted to share her moment of pride:

she was not nor ever had been a murderer; and she had changed the law. She was released immediately to the large, euphoric crowd outside in the Strand.

A young woman who had been imprisoned since she was 18, who had lived so much of her life in institutions, or on the wing, suddenly found herself free. No institutions or services were responsible for her. The women's movement had claimed her, but did she want to be in that movement? Triumph confronted the campaign with a crisis: where was Emma Humphreys to live? How was she to live? By appealing she was cut off by the prison service from the pre-release preparation that would have connected her with a network of public services – welfare, health, housing and employment – to help her transition from an institutionalised life to an autonomous life. Harriet Wistrich recalled that, unsusprisingly, "Emma couldn't really cook. She could make a sandwich."

Since her late teens, Emma had not only lived in an institution, but the purpose of her incarceration was – precisely – to strip her of self-determination: planning a day, eating, earning, cleaning, shopping, travelling, making decisions had no longer been her responsibility. Not only had she been deprived of the social skills necessary to everyday life *in* the world, but before her imprisonment her personal economy had engaged her in the most intimate exploitation of her very person: her selfhood had been up for sale. She was not prepared for a sustainable personal economy. When Emma mutinied against a multiple threat to her person, killing someone to save herself, she landed up in a controlled environment that was, paradoxically, unfree and yet safe. But the conditions of that problematic safety also, ultimately, cost Emma Humphreys her life. Her physical and mental health had been subdued in prison by medication – high doses of toxic medication, to which she became, unsurprisingly, addicted.

However, even at the beginning of her relationship to Justice for Women, it was clear to Julie Bindel that Emma was a profoundly needy woman. Following a disastrous home leave visit from open prison, ending in rape and an overdose and then a serious cutting up episode in Holloway prison, Justice for

Women decided that she needed more support than the campaign group were able to offer her. So it was that Linda Regan volunteered to befriend Emma, to become someone who would visit her in prison, regularly, come what may, to offer a confidential space in which she could air her feelings about anything. Regan has never disclosed the content of their conversations, but she has discussed the importance to Emma of finding a facility strong enough and humane enough to hold her, to begin to sort out the stuff in her life story that remained unresolved, a catastrophic pain. As the appeal approached, Linda set about organising a secure placement in a mental health community to support Emma if the appeal succeeded and she was released. But they had been unable to find a place for her immediately.

So, when Emma Humphreys emerged from the back of the court into the arms of the crowd in the Strand there was an urgent problem: where was she to live? How was she to take care of herself? Indeed, how was she to *be?* Was she herself clear and confident? Was the campaign more than a resource for her release and the revelation of what might drive a woman to kill another human being? Was it – could it ever be – a home? "Justice for Women had been very clear," says Harriet Wistrich, "it was a two way thing – we were campaigning for *her*, and we asked of her a willingness to work with the media. That was a strain for her, though she didn't shy away from it. And once we took her on a feminist march in Manchester quite early after her release, and she really enjoyed that. She was keen to do that."

But there was also another constituency wanting to claim Emma. Behind that crowd and that joy in the Strand there was a spectre: the men who had great expectations of this little woman. Several had been writing to her in prison. In the absence of a discharge plan, Emma was released into what must have seemed like an empty space. She was uncomfortable in an ordinary house – having spent her life in institutions or temporary bed and breakfast accommodation, or on the street, she was unsettled by a house that was also a home. She was desperate to do what she knew how to do: get herself down to Kings Cross where she could score men and money and heroin.

Within a couple of weeks Emma went to the therapeutic community, but that didn't last long. There she was suddenly faced with responsibilities that she'd been deprived of for so long in prison – responsibility for her own life. She came back to London where she stayed with Julie and Harriet until she found her own bedsit, dressed up for Kings Cross, scored men and heroin, and drank any alcohol she could find in the house. "All along we had been helping her fight authority, and suddenly we were authority," says Harriet Wistrich, "I don't think she knew how to be, or who she was. I think the prostitution was something she could do. The reality of having freedom was such that she needed to blot her brains out."

Emma's friends in the campaign tried to remain faithful, stayed in touch, organised days out, but they also became exasperated with her excess, the drinking, the drugs, the men. Eventually Emma herself seemed to grasp how dangerous her life was becoming when she was raped in a hostel by a man who had apparently befriended her.

Life settled into a precarious routine. Every week she joined Harriet and Julie and Rosie for Sunday lunch. She didn't really eat – they'd prepared her favourite pitta bread sandwich. That was their routine, too, for three Christmases. But though her life became calmer, and she stopped putting herself into situations in which she was endangered by men, her engagement with life was ebbing: she remained so heavily medicated that sometimes she struggled to stay awake; her anorexia was so severe that her body was shrinking, her weight was below five stone.

Everyone was worried when, for a couple of days in July 1998 her friends tried telephoning and they couldn't raise a reply. Harriet Wistrich and Julie Bindel called by her little flat on their way to Rosie's hairdressing salon on Saturday morning. There was no answer when they knocked. They had keys, they opened up and found her: she was dead. The inquest concluded: death by misadventure.

Beatrix Campbell and Judith Jones

I loved

I loved my cell,
I made it my home.
A washroom to bathe,
In a blue plastic bowl.
No potty but a toilet,
An instant disposal.
Beautiful pictures on the walls,
Hours of looking and admiring.
A comfortable corner,
For music, drugs and dreaming.
A bedroom always in use,
To sleep, doss or make love in.

Holloway, July 1994

Nothing to Show

There is nothing to show, no evidence.
A few photos here and there.
Oh, a few scars, but I've almost done it.
It is ten years, ten years of nothing, a waste.
But this head is full.
Not from prison.

5th September 1994

Emma in East Sutton Park prison, 1993.

4: Letters from Prison

This chapter contains a selection of letters written to Justice for Women by Emma in the lead-up to her appeal. They reveal the strength and confidence that Emma gained from having a political context and a campaign group to validate her. They show the struggles she had within the prison system when her battle for freedom started coming into conflict with the prison rules and the philosophy of the prison service lifer unit. They also reveal something of the day-to-day life of a life-sentence prisoner, and of Emma's friendships and love affairs.

Emma was sentenced 'to be detained at Her Majesty's pleasure', an indeterminate life sentence that is mandatory for all people under the age of 18 who are convicted of murder. The Home Secretary set her 'tariff' at eight years, although she was not informed of the length of her sentence until February 1995, following a House of Lords ruling that required all mandatory lifers to be informed of their tariff. The tariff is the minimum sentence a lifer must serve 'in order to satisfy the requirement of retribution and deterrence' before they are eligible for release on life licence. Even once released on licence, a life-sentence prisoner will never be entirely free, and can always be subject to recall to prison should she breach the conditions of her license. The parole board assesses eligibility for release on licence, taking into account such factors as the lifer's disciplinary record and whether they have participated in appropriate courses to challenge their offending behavior. The parole board may recommend a lifer for release on licence only if they are satisfied that the prisoner is no longer a danger to the public.

Thus, when Emma contacted us, even though she was approaching the final stage of her imprisonment, she still had to satisfy the parole board that she was ready for release, and that, if released, she would conform with the conditions of her licence. However, in embarking on an appeal at this late stage, and in choosing to run with a high-profile campaign, she came into conflict with the parole process. First, in challenging her murder conviction, questions would inevitably be raised as to whether she was showing appropriate remorse and was properly addressing her 'offending behaviour'. Second, in giving interviews to the press and generally adopting a more confrontational stance in relation to the prison system, her prison 'discipline record' would be seen in a less favourable light by the prison authorities.

On 6 June 1994 (nine years into her sentence), Emma received the following memorandum from the Lifer Unit:

> The secretary of state has referred your case to the Parole Board which has not recommended your release on licence for the following reasons:
> 'The Parole Board considered that in her present and vulnerable state Miss Humphrey presents too great a risk for open prison or release on licence. The panel recommended an early review in view of her good progress in the past and noted that she could do so again and could be moved quickly through the system.'
> In these circumstances the Secretary of State has no power to release you at this stage. The next formal review will begin in May 1995.

So why did Emma embark on the campaign and appeal at such a late stage in her prison sentence? The answer may be partly found in the letters that she wrote from prison. Beyond freedom, Emma craved justice. For her, the need to overcome the stigma of being labeled a murderer (and for the rest of her life being free only on licence) became more important than achieving immediate release from prison.

The first letter included here was written by Emma from Drake Hall prison to the Justice for Women campaign. Drake Hall is an open prison. Female lifers can only progress to open prison once they have successfully completed two previous stages of high-secure and medium-secure prison. The purpose of open prison is to help prisoners start to prepare for their eventual rehabilitation into society, and to test that they are in fact ready for release from prison. Whilst in open prison, inmates are allowed out on temporary release ('TR') to visit family members and gain employment experience.

This first letter was received a few days after the release from prison of Kiranjit Ahluwalia. Kiranjit's campaign for an appeal and her subsequent retrial received extensive media coverage as a result of the work of Southall Black Sisters, who were supported by Justice for Women.

24-9-92   Drake Hall prison, Staffordshire

Dear Julie Bindel, (Justice for Women),
I hope you don't mind me writing to you. I'll try to keep this brief because you're probably very busy – but I'll tell you the basic outline of my case, which I am looking for *any* help . . .

In Dec 85 I was convicted of murdering my boyfriend, Trevor Armitage, who was 35. I had met him six months previously when I was 16 – I was a prostitute and he was a client. I was 17 at the time of the offence and am 24 now.

I moved in with Trevor because I needed somewhere to live and I thought he would look after me.

One night I was raped by three men (reported to police) and that destroyed me. Afterwards I had great difficulty sleeping with Trevor – which he turned into a "punishment" for me.

In my time with Trevor I became very depressed and an alcoholic. I lived on my nerves. I had crawled out of a window a few times after being abused and as a consequence all the escapable windows were nailed shut.

I believed I loved Trevor and stayed with him and put up with the abuse because he always told me he loved me.

Briefly – the night of the offence I had a knife in my hand from cutting my wrists, because I wanted some kind of response from him other than physical abuse or rape again – as I heard him coming I panicked that maybe he could actually turn even worse and turn the knife on me – and I was cornered upstairs – so I hid my cut arms and put the knife under my leg. He never saw what I had done. He came and laid beside where I was sitting – he was undressed and I knew I was going to be raped again, beaten or both. I couldn't go through it again – I just wanted him to get away from me. In an instant I turned and stabbed him once – and he died as a result.

I got help, the police came and I was arrested. I had no legal or guardian help whilst making my statements, and really I was in no state to carry on a decent conversation and I didn't want to explain some of the abuse and things, so the police "helped" me make my statements – which at the time was an easy way out for me not to have to explain things fully – but the statements ended up not being the full truth.

I was eventually given a duty solicitor whom I had great difficult relating to – and some things I just couldn't talk properly to him about – maybe because he was a man.

I was far from ready for my trial – I couldn't even speak on a one-to-one basis to anyone about how my crime came about, let alone a packed courtroom. So I wouldn't talk in the witness box – but I thought at least my defence lawyers would tell the court the things I had told them. But they didn't. No-one told me they couldn't read it straight out on my behalf – so *nothing* came out – and I was found guilty of murder. It was all just so wrong – and even at that time I was feeling such guilt I didn't care about my life.

You might probably be wondering "why after so long fight your case?" Well – only the last couple of years have I been able to talk to people about my life and offence – and only recently have I gained confidence and courage to do something about what I feel very strongly about – and from my *heart* I believe I didn't deserve this life sentence.

My time in prison hasn't been a bed of roses – I've had to really work on my self-confidence, self-abuse (now conquered!) and I have battled with anorexia for many years. I am not begging for sympathy, I am just trying to let you get a picture of me.

I really do want to take my case back to court. I have a father and Nan in this country who do all they can to help me get through my sentence, but as far as my offence is concerned I have no support, they "don't want to know".

I really need some support.

Thank you for your time,

Emma Humphreys

Julie wrote back, promising to visit and telling Emma how compelled we were by her story. Julie asked her to write again with more details about her background, and about how she was treated by the police and courts, her lawyers and psychiatrists. By return of post, Emma wrote with more details of her case:

Emma Humphreys
P32063
H.M. Prison Drake Hall
Eckleshall
Stafford
ST21 6LQ

4-10-92

Dear Julie Bindel,
Thank you for your letter and saying you will help me in any way you can.

I have just written to my solicitor authorising him to give you any information that you need. I received a letter from him on Friday informing me that he still hasn't received my file, so he is really unable to say whether he feels anything can be done for me until he sees my papers.

I've told you a brief history of my life before I met Trevor. An affidavit was read out at my trial which had come from a social worker in Canada, so that must be somewhere in my file. I have some history sheets here and I agree with most things, but they mention 'drug and alcohol abuse' which I think is an overstatement. I experimented with all drugs while a teenager – after trying them all I left them alone. I never had addictions until a few months before my arrest, and that was alcohol.

After returning to Canada in May 84 I was refused re-admission and left the country willingly in June 84. I then returned to Notts and lived with my gran for a couple of months, until I walked out late one night with about 12p to my name and nowhere to go as I only knew my gran and dad in this country.

I met a woman who took me back to where she was staying, so I stayed with her for one or two weeks. I had no job and wasn't signing on the social, so I went back to prostitution. After a couple of nights working I met Trevor as a punter, I was needing somewhere to stay and he offered me to live with him. He told me that he had been living with a woman, but they were broken up and she was taking her time moving out of the house, so he had been staying at his parents' pub. I stayed in the pub with Trevor for a few days, but his parents didn't want me there, so we moved in to a hotel for a couple of days to give his ex-girlfriend time to move out of the house.

This initial period with Trevor was fine. I continued to work and keep my money. I looked upon him as a full-time client, and in return I was hoping he would look after me and give me a roof over my head.

I never looked past the present day and never expected Trevor to want anything more from me than sex, because no one ever had.

I can't remember exactly when things started to go bad,

but they did soon after we moved in the house together. I didn't really think of us as having a relationship, but he started questioning me about what I had done at work and what people I had met while I was out, this was when he started to hit me. Soon I came to recognise when he was going to go into a rage because he'd go very quiet first.

I started to drop my money earned from each client off at the pub where he was just so I wasn't carrying it around all night. I never saw any of this again and never dared ask for it, I just used to tell him when I needed more Durex for work, stockings or some drink. When I knew I wanted to go shopping the next day I wouldn't drop my money off, calculate how much money should be there, but I would tell him what I wanted to buy. He would leave the money alone, but sometimes after keeping my money I would come downstairs in the morning and my bag would be empty.

He'd started to get paranoid I was saving up to go back to live in Canada with my friend Susan. I had to be at his side or at home by 11.00/11.30, but sometimes I couldn't do this so I would get beat up, most of the beatings were work-orientated . . . he hadn't seen me out all that night, as he used to always drive around to see what I was up to, or the money didn't add up to how long I'd worked, or I'd just mention somebody I'd met.

Usually he'd punch me about the head, except once when I thought I was pregnant he kicked and punched me in the stomach instead. Once he sat with a knife and told me he would cut up my face so I would be ugly, but I left the house before he came back downstairs.

I would always ask him "why"? After he hit me and he'd just say "because I love you" and I believed him, because he wasn't always horrible to me, and the situation reminded me of my mom at home, and he'd cry and say sorry.

When he went to bed at night he would lock both doors, so a couple of times I crawled out of the little kitchen window and would go and stay in a hotel, but I would always go back. Sometimes the same night I would phone him to come and pick me up, or the next day.

I did feel like I loved him, but I think I loved him because he loved me and I always wanted someone to love me, but the only times he told me he loved me was after a fight or in bed.

When in Canada, since a young age I had cut my wrists when things got tough; it was my way of getting a response from someone and to let people know I was upset. One time after a bad fight I asked to go to the toilet, and when I did I cut my wrists. For about three days afterwards Trevor never picked arguments or hit me, it seemed to make him stop and think for a while, but it didn't last.

One night at work I was taken by a man to an empty flat where two other men appeared, they took it in turns to rape me while they held a pair of pointed scissors. I didn't want any violence or even to be killed, so I didn't fight them off. I just hoped that if I let them do what they wanted they would let me go, and they did.

One man drove me to the city centre and there I got a taxi straight home, and the taxi driver stopped at a shop to get me a bottle of vodka. I phoned Trevor as soon as I got home, I wouldn't tell him over the phone but he said he would come straight home, but he didn't.

Afterwards I had terrible feelings about myself about not fighting them off, although at the time I thought it best to co-operate. I couldn't understand why they would pick a prostitute to rape, or anyone to rape when men can go to a club or pub and get a one-night stand, but mostly I regretted not fighting them off. I let it happen even though I didn't want it to happen.

I phoned my mom in Canada and talked to her about it but I didn't feel any better about it all. I didn't want to talk to Trevor about it. By the time he got home I was double hurting, because he hadn't come home when I needed him.

I never reported the rape directly to the police because being a prostitute I knew I wouldn't get much sympathy, but I was concerned for the other girls so I spread the word to watch out for these men. Eventually the police came to me for a statement in which I just told the facts – it was all they wanted. They asked me if I would give evidence in court if they were arrested and I said no. No one told me that if I didn't give evidence they would never be charged with raping me, which still annoys me now, but I know now they were charged with raping someone else.

I continued to work although I hated it, but I just kept going. Sleeping with Trevor became a trauma – I hated it – even though I used to try, but I would leave the bed to be sick. I thought I was going mad. I told my mom when I phoned her, but she told me it's normal. As soon as I started refusing Trevor sex he would force me. I was told on occasions, "naughty little girls must pay for what they do wrong," and be forced to have sex, sometimes along with being punched and dragged around the house by my hair. Other times he'd just force me, with no hitting or telling me I was a naughty little girl. I hated these words as much as what he did.

I still loved him, but the more he kept forcing me to have sex and hitting me I felt worse with myself, and used to wait in dread of the next confrontation.

I'd been given bail for a number of charges of soliciting, loitering, two assaults that took place on Christmas day in a hotel, and then before I left Trevor's house one day and I did criminal damage on the house. Trevor had me charged because I had been leaving him and also he thought a man had also done it, but this charge was dropped when I told Trevor I was going back to live with him. I stayed in a bail hostel until I breached my bail, and then spent three weeks on remand. Trevor was at court and I walked out with a two-year conditional discharge and a fine.

I was happy to be out of Risley, and I still loved Trevor because even though he treated me bad he was the only one who cared about me, but I was a bag of nerves because I knew what I was going back to. This was Thursday.

I can't remember why, but he beat me on the living-room

floor on Friday night, then left the house. I phoned my mom in Canada and told her I had to get away. She promised to phone someone in London to find me somewhere to go and phone me back, but she never got back to me because Trevor came home and locked the phone out in the car and locked up the house and went to bed. I then found out the windows were nailed shut.

Saturday night I was picked up by the Vice squad again which Trevor was mad about. I told him I didn't want to go back to work again that night, so we went to a club then back to his parents' pub. I pleaded with him to let me go to my gran's for a couple of weeks for a break, but he didn't want this even though I told him I would leave most of my things with him and would come straight back, so in the end he said OK. When I phoned my gran she refused to have me, so he took me home and we went out. I refused to go to bed with him.

Sunday night I stayed out late, because I was waiting at my friend Neil Jones' flat waiting for him to come home. I wanted to leave Trevor, I was afraid to go home, but when Neil didn't show up I went home and refused to sleep with Trevor again.

Monday night Trevor came home at about 5.30pm and he got annoyed when I told him the police had been at the house, but I didn't speak to them because I didn't know what they wanted. He left the house and sent a taxi to the house to take me to work.

I did one customer who thought we were being followed, so he dropped me next to a taxi. I didn't have the right money to give the taxi driver so I suggested we go into the pub and buy a drink, then I could give him the money. So we did this, but Trevor came into the pub. I panicked because I was supposed to be working. I got rid of the taxi driver and tried to sweeten Trevor up and said I would go round with him for the rest of the night, but I knew I was in for trouble.

Trevor was with his son, who was fifteen or sixteen years old, and a friend Martin. On the way to the car he suggested to the other two to gang-bang me. I didn't want to get into the back of the car, I didn't want to get into the car at all, but I did and they never did it. We went into another pub where I sat talking to his son, Steven. Trevor was in a very bad mood; he was making loud comments about me refusing to sleep with him, and threw the car and house keys at his son because he was thinking how I wanted to sleep with his son. His son drank my drink, I felt so sick with nerves, I couldn't even drink.

Trevor, his son and I went back to the house. They wanted to watch TV, so I went upstairs with some music and a drink of neat vodka.

Now things were coming to boiling point with Trevor. I'd been back four days and hadn't let him sleep with me; I still loved him and wanted to please him. I sat and listened to music and touched up my make-up. I really wanted to please him and to keep the peace, but I felt sick inside and couldn't even drink what I wanted. I felt like a wreck. I was so afraid of what was going to happen that night because I still hadn't been punished for being sat in the pub with the taxi driver, but I didn't want to be hit or forced into sex.

Trevor called up to say he was driving his son home. I didn't plan it or think too long about it, but I thought if I make a dramatic scene when he comes home he will be good to me. So I rushed downstairs and got a knife from the kitchen, but I wanted him to think I was really serious about killing myself so I took two knives back upstairs with me. I wanted to divert his mind away from wanting to punish me with violence or forced sex. So I cut my wrists and sat there on the landing waiting for him to come home. As soon as I heard him come in the door I panicked, what if he turned one of the knives on me? What if me having cut my wrists made him even more angry? I had no time before he came up the stairs to do anything so I just thought of hiding what I'd done, so I put the knives under my legs and put my arms down and pulled my sleeves down.

Trevor came upstairs and went past me into the bedroom

and came out again dressed only in his shirt; I knew then it wasn't just a beating to come. He lay beside me where I was sitting and with his bottom part next to me. He never saw my wrists cut or the knives, he lay there silent but this wasn't unusual before he started on me.

I was terrified. I was on the landing cornered upstairs by someone who was about to abuse me and two knives. I couldn't take it anymore I just wanted him to get away from me, and I don't know what I believed he was going to do, I never looked I just turned, pulled one of the knives out and stabbed him.

Straight away I couldn't believe what I'd done. I got mad at him initially, but only for a few seconds. Something inside told me it was serious, although upon arrest I couldn't have told you where the stab wound was or that there was any blood.

Don't ask me why, but inside I knew he was dying and going to die. He stood up and said "Oh God" and then fell down. I held him and cried and talked to him. Then I needed to get help so I went out into the street and flagged down a car.

The rest isn't very clear except I remember them not letting me go into see him, which I wanted to do. I didn't really want to leave him to go and get help, I didn't want to leave him alone but he needed help and the thought of death terrified me.

The police came and I was arrested. I saw a police doctor who took a blood sample and measured any scars or bruises I had. (All the scars were self-inflicted on my arms and I just had a bruise on my wrist from being pinned down on the Friday night). Apparently my alcohol level was zero.

I was in a terrible state but they wanted a police statement. When I answered, "I don't know or I can't remember", they wanted more, but I really didn't feel up to talking. So things were suggested to me that 'might' have happened at the time – it felt easier just to agree with these things than go into great detail, because I knew they wouldn't understand. I can't remember all of my statement, but here are the things that aren't true.

1. I said I meant to kill him: all I meant to do was stop him from hurting me that night. I would never intentionally seriously hurt anyone. I was made to feel like I must have meant to kill him, and because I had never killed anyone before I sat there and half believed I did, but I didn't.

2. When they kept asking why, I kept saying, "I don't know", because there was too much behind why and I didn't want to talk about it. So suggestions were made to me as why, and I ended up agreeing to Trevor supposedly teasing me about not having cut my wrists very good. This is *so* far from the truth. *No way* did he see the knives or my cut wrists or even speak one word before I stabbed him. I felt they wanted an 'instant' reason why.

3. I said in my statements that Trevor and I lived together but agreed not to have sex. This is also not true. I said this so they would stop going on at me about why he had no clothes on, that was the last thing I wanted to talk about.

4. The police wanted to know, "why two knives?". I told them to cut my wrists but they suggested that they could have been used to protect myself, which of course is true. But I am not someone who uses knives on people or anything. When I took those knives out of the drawer, the only thing on my mind was Trevor being convinced I would kill myself because I was fed up with it all. I wanted a dramatic scene for him to make him stop and think. It *never* entered my head to use them on anyone but myself.

5. I denied he was my ponce/*forced* me to be a prostitute because I was one when I met him. But he did get all of my money, he didn't really need it but he was afraid of me saving to leave him.

I would go on the lie detector over these things because they are not true.

You must be thinking now that I'm some sort of complete idiot, well, I admit I was. I didn't want to go into the complete story, and when suggestions were made I agreed because of not wanting to talk, and I thought the police knew what they were on about; it was just an easy way out.

The police got me a solicitor, Mr D. Donegan, who came when I was formally charged.

I spent eleven months on remand at Risley. I couldn't relate to my solicitor very well at all, and one thing that really annoyed and upset me was that he kept telling me: "Trevor was no good anyway." I didn't want to hear that. I still believed I loved him, and I'd killed the person I thought loved me.

Do you know – I don't ever remember him asking me "why?" or really wanting to know why. I felt he wanted to build-up on what I'd said in my police statements and just hear about physical beatings off Trevor.

I didn't have confidence in Mr Donegan and I had no confidence in myself, fifty per cent of the time I just wanted to be tried and given life and be left alone.

I kept telling him I couldn't speak up in court in the box. He said if I did I could get just a couple of years and then he said he could get me a job in a country club where I could work as a prostitute again.

I think sometimes I was trying to come across as being all together and happy with all my life, but the last thing I wanted to be free for was to go back to selling my body.

I can't remember the first psychiatrist I saw, but apparently it didn't agree with diminished responsibility. Mr Donegan wanted me to see a second one, and he said he hoped the psychiatrist would put down that I had some sort of "psychopathic tendencies", those were his words. This was to me a label used for really over-the-top mad people, I wasn't mad. I was terrified of saying too much to the second psychiatrist. I can also remember Mr Donegan sitting there and saying, "you and I both know you are crazy".

The only thing that kept me going on remand were my solicitor's visits, not for any other reason than he was my only visitor and he brought me up my cigarettes, wine, chocolate, some earrings and clothes.

I wrote to my friend Neil and told him I wasn't happy with my solicitor, so he got me in contact with another. He came for a visit and wanted to take on my case, so that's what I wanted. A few days later I was called for another special visit and thought it was the new one, but it was Mr Donegan. I felt guilty for wanting to change solicitors and he told me we were so close to trial to get it over and done with; he also brought me my goodies so I kept him.

My trial came – but I knew there was no way I could ever begin to say my police statements were lies, because I am not a liar usually and I don't like liars and then I would have had to go into the real why.

I *really* didn't want to go into why I couldn't sleep with him anymore – and how he would call me "a naughty little girl". And I was *so* ashamed to say I couldn't stand the sex because I thought I was abnormal – and being a prostitute, I thought I would be laughed at and no one would ever understand. I couldn't talk to people, and to stand in the witness box and tell such personal things just haunted me.

The only defence witness was the second psychiatrist I saw, the rest were prosecution witnesses but I can't remember anyone saying anything bad about me. And a statement from Canadian Social Services was read out.

I did go into the witness box, but only answered my name and address, and I think that was it; I couldn't do it and, even worse, I could see one of the knives.

The judge let me talk to my QC again and he tried to make me fight for my life, but just before we were going to go back up he said: "Let me ask you a question, what were you more afraid of before you stabbed him, a beating or the sex?" And I said, "the sex".

From then on I knew I couldn't talk about it all, so I went

182 The Map of My Life

back into the box just to agree that what I said in my police statements were true. The easy way out, and a big mistake maybe for any possible appeal.

An appeal was put in to the "first judge" on two grounds, to do with provocation and what came out of the original trial – there was never any hope, it was turned down and I signed a paper abolishing all appeal proceedings.

I want to also say that I thought even if I didn't go into the witness box my solicitor/QC could read out what I told them; no one told me any different.

I'm sorry this letter has gone on so long, but I wanted you to know what it was all about because I'd never want anyone to take an interest in something they weren't fully aware of. I do know there are a lot of women who have been through a lot more than myself, and I do know what I have done is wrong, but I don't believe I deserve this conviction or sentence.

I must also tell you that last week the prison made quite a big issue about me appealing, and it's been made clear to me that continuing to try for this appeal will jeopardise my future parole reports, as it is interpreted as me not accepting what I've done or my sentence. But I do know what I've done is wrong, but society and the law hasn't tried me on the actual way it was and I think I deserve that.

They interrogated me as an adult, they tried me as an adult, but they sentenced me as a juvenile (H.M.P.), but I've made it clear I am quite prepared to sit here and jeopardise my future parole because I believe in what I'm trying to do.

Sorry this letter is a bit jumbled up.

Thanks for listening.

From Emma

Shortly before Julie was due to visit Emma at Drake Hall prison, she received a phone call from Emma in a very distressed and agitated state. She explained that she had been accused by another inmate of threatening her with a knife and, as a result, was going to be moved from open conditions to Holloway prison whilst the matter was investigated. Emma was adamant that that the allegation was fabricated, and concerned about how bad it would look for her just before Justice for Women were going to take up her case.

H.M.P. Holloway
Parkhurst Rd
London N.7.
4-11-92

Dear Julie,

I'm really sorry about what's happened. But I am *not* guilty of an alleged knife incident.

I have just wrote out a ten-page statement (which no-one seems interested in) – but I hope to get a photocopy to send to you.

I *will* fight this, because whatever has been said about a knife is *not* true.

One minute I feel strong because I *know* what happened. But the next I feel weak because this has come out of the blue, it's bizarre and it *could* wreck my life – when it was going so well.

But this S.D., and whoever, if anyone, put her up to this, knew the impact of such a lie. I will fight this – if I can fight my conviction I can do this, but it's come at a bad time and I didn't need extra hassle.

I am getting knocked down – but I will come up stronger.

Please don't believe this knife business – it's not me.

No way am I an idiot to jeopardise me being in an open prison *or* jeopardise fighting my case.

Please continue your support as this will never stand at the end of the day. I think I desperately need a solicitor. Should I contact Rohit about this matter – or someone else?

Sorry this isn't a very good letter – but my head is wrecked. I would desperately like to talk to you – I don't know if you could visit. But please, give me some advice about what solicitor or who to contact. I think this is too serious (because of my position in fighting my case) for just prison and M.P. complaints – I will do those also though, if I should.

I will do nothing more before hearing from you OK – but thought I'd get a statement done because people *must* know what I have to say – and how it's probably come about. Please talk to Christine Wilson my P.O. about me. This is *not* me – and never has been me. I have spoke to her briefly about this on the telephone tonight.

I haven't even been on a prison report since about 1986-7. My only problems being a fight with a girl in '86 (no weapons or anything). I did a sit-in for two hours in H-wing which we all got fines for, and that's it.

My problems in the past in prison have been with eating disorders (which I've had since the age of 15) and wrist slashing, which you know about – and which stopped about five years ago now.

I have also suffered with P.M.T. for a very long time – probably due to my eating problem. But I've sought and am receiving help for that. But, I have never suffered "angry feelings" of P.M.T. – just depressed and suicidal – which I can deal with now, understanding what it is. This allegation is outrageous.

I do hope you can support me through this.

There was *no hint* of "official trouble" before this or these allegations. I was due to go on an overnight stay or day release next Thursday 12th – to talk to family and friends about my offence and the whole case – and I'd been recommended my first home leave for Xmas – and had been doing on town visits since July – with *no* problems.

I don't know what else to tell you. I have no idea what to say to my family – although I will write to a couple of friends tonight.

Please write soon.

Emma Humphreys – P32063
H.M. Prison Holloway
13-11-92

Dear Julie,
It was nice to finally meet you today – I think the work you're all doing is great. Once again, thanks for your support.

I've enclosed some letters of response from the press and like – I will also write to Irene Macmillan at Rough Justice to ask her to send the file or copy to you when she receives it. I think I have already authorised Chris Wilson to give you any info you need.

I really don't know what to write for you like you asked – but if I ask myself why I think I should have an appeal heard, it's because:

1) I was convicted really on my police statement which was 'far from the truth of things';

2) Eight years ago I couldn't talk about things which distressed me;

3) I was afraid to relate some of the things I'd been feeling – and knew just 'cause I was a prostitute there wouldn't be much sympathy coming my way.

I really don't want to slag off my solicitor, but he was definitely the wrong person and I think getting to the bottom of things was too much hard work for him. I want to be judged on how it actually was for me – and how it came about – and if that was heard I don't think I'd have a murder conviction.

If that's any use to you – maybe you could sort it out into better terms.

All my life I was very unhappy, very shy and had no self-confidence, but that was because I didn't like me or my life. The most important thing I've learned is to 'accept' me, 'like' me and work for a better future. But I want to put the past to rest PROPERLY. I'm not afraid or ashamed to speak out anymore, because I like me – no matter what anyone thinks – and most of all I believe in me.

I know fighting this conviction is not going to be easy – but

I am prepared for that – and to put all my effort into it.

I am seriously going to talk to the lifer liaison officer here to see about staying here – if they can swing it with the Home Office to allow me my day releases and home leaves from here. And would definitely fight to come out to do some work for you.

I've just spent all afternoon sorting this room out – I was very reluctant to move up here last night – but I actually prefer it now I've had all my pictures up (I'm a great fan of Marilyn Monroe and fantasy pictures). If it wasn't for being here through this alleged incident, I'd be happy to be here, because I've settled well. But I'm sure why I'm here will be brushed under the carpet at the end of the day.

I've never met women like I came across on my house at Drake – it was actually hell – so if this allegation doesn't continue, I've come out of it 'TOPS'.

I'll close for now – and look forward to seeing you again.

Take care.

Em.

Emma was eventually cleared of the knife incident, and remained at Holloway prison for a few months before being transferred to another open prison. In the meantime, her proximity at HMP Holloway enabled regular visits from Justice for Women. Rohit Sanghvi, the solicitor who had acted for Kiranjit Ahluwalia, agreed to take on Emma's case, and Harriet offered to act as Emma's main contact and to assist the legal case by preparing a detailed background statement. Additionally, Justice for Women started to build-up the campaign, in particular by setting up interviews with the media.

Emma Humphreys – H.M. Prison Holloway
Friday pm

Dear Julie and Harriet,
Thanks for all you're doing for me.

I hope I didn't sound ungrateful on the phone tonight. Inside you know I'm very happy. At last I have what I wanted – people listening, helping me and supporting my fight to be tried fairly of how I've ended in prison and why I've come to be writing to you now.

I suppose sometimes in the past when I've thought about "going back to court" I've never really looked past dingy cold legal visits – and just really like my last court case. I suppose I never looked at feeling like people do actually care about *me* and want to listen and help me – and not just people doing a job – ordinary people.

And then you get to feeling: "Look at all this support I'm getting – do I deserve this when if all the energy and time taken up on helping me was channeled into helping abused kids or groups of people suffering, there would be more than one person happy at the end of the day."

But I say to myself, my own pain will pay off for other women now and in the future.

And I think maybe I feel like you've accepted I'm not as together as maybe some of the other women you help are, and I've loads of insecurities – a bit of a pill head (although I've had one instead of five today) and just me.

I didn't get to see the news tonight – or hear the radio bits – but if you say it's going good, then I know it is.

Sara [Thornton] probably thinks I'm an ignorant cow – still haven't wrote to her and many other people. Must put her a few lines in the post tomorrow to say I'll write soon.

My Dad's upset me, not sending the rose and card – but I'll write over the weekend.

Charleen [girlfriend in prison at the time] went home this morning. I treated her like shit for the past week. But still – she was there till the last minute – and now the wait to see if she forgets me. (POSITIVE THINKING FOR YOU!)

Oh! – I think today's just a crap day – I need to put on some "cry eye" music and have a cry.

Today – P.M.S. and spots, Charleen leaving, my soulmate Nicky not being here, trying to cut the tablets, feeling fat and basically a shit day!

But the ending of today was OK – Nicky came back from her two-day release with some presents for me – (I'm a Marilyn Monroe fan) – she couldn't find a M.M. mug so she go me one of the latest books – and two posters AND – what more could I ask for the day Charleen left? . . . a troll doll with long red hair, big eyes, false boobs and red and black underwear!

What about Trevor's family in all this – wouldn't it be OK to have especially his son informed about me fighting for an appeal? I *know* it's not very nice for them.

I'll wait – and if you think it's good for me to go back to open, I will. Sometimes I want to – sometimes I don't – mostly I know I'm settled here with friends, and I need to be settled to go through all this – but we'll see.

Well – I'll go for now and see you in the week and Friday.

Yes – it's OK about the Notts television thing and the other one – I know you'll do what's best. Look how Radio 1 turned out – I think it's all going to go good.

Remember to thank Rohit and everyone else working for me.

I'm fine here – really.

Take care of yourselves.

Bye.

Love

Em XXX

In the Spring of 1993 Emma was returned to open prison, this time HMP East Sutton Park in Kent (known as 'ESP' by the inmates). She was again given temporary release, and together Harriet and Emma went shopping in the local town and met with a TV crew to give an interview for BBC Nottingham. Emma was then permitted a long weekend to travel up to Nottingham to see her father and younger sister, who was visiting from Canada. At the end of the emotional visit, Emma had to make her way back to Kent by train on her own. She arrived at Kings Cross, but there she was picked up by a man who sexually abused her. She took an overdose and ended up back in Holloway. She clearly felt horrified by her 'failure', and retreated into self-harm and the oblivion of any drugs that she could get her hands on. At that time heroin was rife within the prison, and Emma tried this drug for the first time in her life. A year later, she reflected on her experience.

Written April 94
It was July/August time. I was totally screwed up, depressed and desperate within myself to try to figure out how I ended up letting a disgusting creature have all kinds of sex with me. It was horrible, and I knew that as soon as he was finished I would take an overdose. The overdose was the beginning of June.

And you know what? The guilt over my offence became so much more intense again. All I could see was me living this life and always failing, forever full of pain.

I couldn't believe, understand or accept that I had just spent the past eight-and-a-half years in prison for the death of a man who wanted sex with me, then went out and on my first home leave and let another man have me as a toy.

I was disgusted with myself. I had learnt nothing, I felt. But I don't kick myself around about it anymore. Well I do, but not as bad as before.

Believe it or not, I try to believe that everything in my life is for a reason. I try to put that awful night into sense by telling myself that I needed a shock treatment to remind myself I am still vulnerable, and out there I am insecure. I left off put there as a very unhappy girl living a sordid frightening and dangerous life. That's where I left off.

Within these walls all I have learned is superficial. My strength, my confidence . . . This is a different life in here. I've grown to be able to survive my hell life . . . But out there I have a lot to learn.

Yes, I was depressed. Suicidal? Yes. But I don't think my creator wants me to die. My Goddess has never given me the courage to end it all. I am meant to live.

Five days after the overdose I tried heroin for the first time. It was lovely. A peaceful calming drug that put some peace into my head. What I said to my friend that gave it to me was: "Is this what I've been missing for 25 years?" It was a pretty bad time for me to try something new, because I liked it.

I was in a right state. Chasing around the jail for every bit of heroin I could find. I was also compulsively washing. I always felt dirty. Inside and out.

Through this time I took Valium, speed, coke and E . . . anything I could get my hands on. I also had a one-night stand with someone else's girl. I kicked myself about that also, because since Charleen went home I had not been with anyone . . . no-one was good enough. Then I lowered myself to that. So my life was shit everywhere I turned.

I was having severe depression before a period. I guess it seemed worse with all the shit in my life. And after not cutting up for so many years, I resorted back to it.

What I had really wanted to do was destroy my insides. My own head was in war. A rational side of me was not wanting to destroy my chances of giving birth to a child one day, but the other side of me was wanting to destroy my insides. No more periods, no more sex with a man. I was at the lowest state of mind I'd been in for a long time.

When it was evening and we were locked in, I put myself in the corner of my room. With an emery board I sharpened a little red knife I had, and, the quietest I could, I broke a glass jar.

What was I thinking of? I thought of slicing my abdomen

open and taking out all my womanly bits and pieces. Then I would get help. I just wanted the part of me that gives me so much grief, gone.

I thought of stabbing myself inside with the knife.

That night I sat in the corner for ages trying to get the courage up to do those things. All I ended up with was a superficial cut on my abdomen. And after trying to put force behind the knife inside of me, I gave up. So, I was even a failure to myself.

I cried, I sobbed, I felt so much pain in my heart and head. A failure to myself, I got into bed with a piece of glass and cut my arms up. Some time I fell asleep.

H.M. Prison
Holloway
Thursday night

Dear Harriet and Julie,
It was good seeing you again today Harriet – thanks for coming – and I hope you feel OK about the visit.

Sorry it was cut short. I'm putting a complaint in tomorrow about being frog-marched off the visit. It was *not* any bloody wing cleaners' meeting, they wanted me upstairs – strip-searched and every nook and cranny of my room. How dare the cheeky fuckers do that? Stop my visit for that.

I went hysterical as soon as they wanted me to strip off. Nickie was next door also about to be stripped – and she started on them then 'cause they had all crowded my room then which made me even madder.

I was 1mm away from really wrecking this room for them and refusing to strip. But I told myself I've had to take my clothes off for plenty of sadistic-minded people while working as a prostitute – so this was just another couple of sick women who willingly try to strip another woman of the privacy of her own body ('cause they'd *never* strip my pride and dignity 'cause I'm too strong) – and ask for a pay-cheque for doing it.

But – my payment – knowing damn well I'm too fast and clever for them to ever pin any illegals on me.

Holloway
Tuesday

Dear Harriet,
How are you? How was your holiday? I hope you had a good time.

I've missed you terribly, honest I've been lost not being able to call you and talk, but I have held it together and I'm still in one piece.

I know I don't write very often, and I never tell you how much I value you being part of my life, but I do. Without you I don't know where I'd be.

You as a person, Julie as a person, you've been and are half my sanity through all this, and I strongly believe that at the end of the day things are going to be OK for me.

You know I strongly believe I shouldn't be in prison, and I believe that when my case is presented to the courts I will be freed. I believe no other, and refuse to even consider any other, and when my freedom comes it won't be the appeal courts I will be thanking.

I know you don't believe in some of my thoughts and feelings on some things and I have been very difficult to work with; you've probably felt like bashing me against a wall at times. Thanks for sitting back and taking deep breaths!

It was good seeing you down probation before your holiday, and I really hadn't wanted the visit at all. Nothing to do with you, but that's how I am when I feel shit about myself and am really on a hate-Emma mission: I can't face people who care about me, because it makes me feel guilty that someone is bothering to care about me and 'cause I always let others down.

I am glad I saw you and the tapes [that Rosie sent] are great, thanks.

Thanks also for your letter and the money you sent before you left.

I haven't started any education or anything yet, I've got to get myself together first. Harriet, I know I've got to start to do things, constructive things, and I am beginning to get myself together, honest.

I am still very sad though, and to be honest with you, if I had the guts I would have ended it long ago. I've so much inside, so much shit, so many emotions that screw up my head. I get all confused and get a feeling like I don't know how to handle it all.

Since your visit, I've been blocking it all out as much as possible and just getting through each day.

I was really low one day last week and I was so close to resorting to what I used to do, closer than I've been since the last time I did it over five years ago. I'm so glad I didn't.

I honestly don't believe I'm a bad person, Harriet, but I really don't like me and I am always so afraid other people won't like me.

Please don't think this is a depressing suicidal letter Harriet, it's not, I'm just trying to tell you bits and pieces.

I've actually loads I'd like to sit down and talk to you about, but you're right, I do need to build-up a good relationship with a counsellor, even if it would be a lot easier to wake up one morning with amnesia and just deal with the day's problems and the future. Anyway, before I start rambling on I'm keen to get a visit from Rohit and the barrister; I know it can't be rushed but I will feel tons better once some appeal grounds are talked through and written up.

I've wanted to tell you what Trevor used to say to me before making me have sex, and the more it became an issue to tell you, the more I got revolted at the thought of his words.

"Naughty girls must pay for what they have done wrong." There you go. It probably doesn't sound anything to you, but even thinking his words makes me want to be sick, bash myself against a wall and wash myself till I'm worn out.

It's not me I hate, not the person so much, Harriet, it's my body maybe, maybe that's where the anorexia comes into it,

I don't know, I'm confused.

The other night when I wanted to 'cut up' it wasn't just my arms, I wanted to cut the whole of my body, and I've never felt like that before. I wanted to mess up my whole body. God, I must be totally fucked up, because although there's part of me I hate, I know I've got a lot of good.

I've a lot of understanding and patience to give to people. I want to do something so worthwhile with my life and some day I want to see my mum happy, but I don't know if she could ever work through her problems and live happy. I'm lucky: out of the two of us, I'm twenty-five and she's fifty odd.

I'm emotionally weak, but some part of me must be strong. I wish I could give some strength to my mother.

Well, guess who turned up last Thursday? Head office (Paul Newall and Mitch Egan) [from the prison service lifer unit]. I couldn't believe it, they had just locked me in over the tea hour and came back and sprung it on me.

We'll probably have to talk about this in detail because there is so much involved in it. I couldn't tell you how it went, I just don't know, but you know what Harriet? At the end of the day I don't feel I owe anyone except *myself* and *my* people an explanation. If the system thought they were doing something good keeping me locked up from when I was seventeen, then when I was twenty five 'expecting' me to cope – on my own – in the middle of a train station after three days of 'freedom' – and everything that went off – they couldn't even start to understand if I tried to explain.

I think I want to talk to you about this, because I need some feedback.

Last week I wrote a letter to the Home Secretary, concerning Holloway being my punishment for not returning to E.S.P. by 8pm and taking the overdose, telling him I didn't think it was right and I would give them a month, twenty-eight days or I would hunger strike and go in segregation. It's here in my room, only you stopped me posting it, I wanted to post it because I'm worn out with everything involved in this sentence and I think they have taken the piss with me.

I also thought about the appeal, I want to be at least as healthy as passed as settled. So don't panic, it won't move from this room until we talk OK? I know you probably won't agree with the letter.

I know I screwed up at the end of my home leave, but you know what? I honestly don't believe Holloway as a punishment is the answer . . . to have the intention of keeping me in closed prison for another three years, then throw me out on home leave again? God, they've no idea.

I better go, 'cause I have loads on my mind and it keeps jumping from one thing to another, and I'm sure already this letter is all mixed up.

I hope you and Julie are OK and I look forward to seeing you soon.

Take care,

Lots of love

Emma x

P.S.

Sorry if it's a screwed up letter, don't worry, I'm OK.

P.P.S.

Nickie has returned again, she was seen down the block yesterday! Also Dawn's on the run from E.S.P!!

The prison service treated Emma's experience whilst on Home Leave as a failure, indicating that she was no longer fit for open conditions and should therefore remain back at Holloway. Justice for Women wrote to the parole board seeking an explanation as to why Emma was denied parole. The parole board replied:

> As you are aware the Board had before them detailed reports of Miss Humphreys. They noted that in November 1992 she was moved from HMP Drake Hall to HMP Holloway following allegations that she had threatened other inmates with a knife on two occasions. She was returned to HMP East Sutton Park in April 1993 and on

28 May 1993 did not return from home leave. She was found in the Kings Cross area on 31 May 1993 having collapsed from taking a quantity of anti-depressants. She claimed she had taken a lift from a man who had raped her.

The Panel, therefore, considered that the two attempts to transfer her to open conditions had failed. She was unable to cope with open conditions and on the second occasion absconded from home leave. When considering a prisoner's suitability for open conditions or release on licence, the risk that he/she may present to the public is of paramount importance to the Board. They were of the opinion that in her present unstable and volatile state she not only presented a risk to the public but also posed a substantive risk to herself.

It was eventually agreed that Emma would remain at Holloway, but be permitted day releases from there. In helping Emma prepare for the Court of Appeal, we arranged a visit with Kiranjit Ahluwalia, so that she could share her experience of a high profile media campaign.

H.M. Prison Holloway
Parkhurst Road London, N7

Dear Harriet,
It was lovely seeing you . . . and you all on Sunday. And I was glad to be going down on the visit letting you see I'm looking and feeling a lot better within myself.

Kiranjit is lovely. I just knew I would like her. When she was talking one-to-one to me, I wanted to break down and cry and just hug her and never let her go. What strength she has. I really admire her and like her, so let her know that before I get her a letter together, which I will send to you and you can pass on to her.

I hope you thanked Julie for the M.M. card, and give her my love. I may see her in here some time this week as she said she was coming in to see someone else.

The counsellor is in tomorrow afternoon. The last session with her was pretty good. It just feels so unnatural to be appointed to talk to someone about serious things, as I usually tend to load all my shit on to people who I sense I can relate to. But I spoke to her and told her that it will take me time to open up to her. Although at the moment I'm finding Jan the most helpful person of all at the moment . . . and see her very regularly.

I eventually got to see Dr Bhatachari [prison doctor] yesterday afternoon to get this P.M.T. treatment sorted out. I didn't feel like discussing all the vomiting and shit, but he weighed me and is keeping an eye on my weight. Anyway, the last two months I was taking a high dose of progesterone for 14 days of the month, and now he has switched me to 200mg of an anti-oestrogen every day of the month. I will take my first one tonight, but before that I will go read up about the treatment in the library later on, I like to know what I'm taking when it comes to 'messing with nature', which I class P.M.T. treatment in.

I have booked a temporary release to have the day out on the 15th or 16th of this month. Are you available for one of those dates? If not, let me know some dates. But I would still like to try for an overnight stay for the 30th, could you handle an all-night bash . . . PARTY TIME!

I'm happy to go ahead with the filming and stuff, but am not keen on any more publicity at the moment. We've got public opinion, we have support. We just have to get to court now.

Even though I dread a courtroom and all the appeal shit, I would very much like to speak up in court. I want to say it all straight from my heart and head and I want to be understood.

I feel confident that given time I will be able to get it across to the judges, in my own words, how Trevor ended up dying. And I feel they will also agree with me that I do not deserve this conviction or sentence. But what I need to do is try to detach my emotions about him as a person and the guilt and pain I feel about his death from the fight with the legal system.

I'll be looking forward to seeing you again, and guess what? I'm in need of more perfume and stamps. So If I'm not seeing you soon, please do me a little treat parcel BUT we are not allowed the pressurised perfume, just the ones you have to 'squirt, squirt' or dab-ons. Yes, it's a fussy prison rule, not mine for once!

How's your studying going? I'm still coming down to computers every day, and am going to start some writing about my life and issues in my head with one of the teachers called Tom.

Off to library . . . BYE . . .

Lots of Love

Em X

In order to build-up the campaign, our main strategy was to attract media coverage, which meant Emma giving interviews to the press, radio and television. Emma was prepared to coop-erate, although this eventually got her into trouble when, during a temporary release day-out from prison, Emma was inter-viewed for a television documentary. On her return to prison, the cameras filmed Emma walking to the gates of Holloway. When asked, she freely told the officers what she had been doing. As a result she lost the privilege of day release. The prison authorities were livid, and as much as they could, they attempted to admonish Justice for Women for leading Emma astray. On many occasions we were led to question ourselves as to whether we serving Emma's best interests. However, Emma was always clear that she wanted a public campaign, even though often it was extremely hard for her to display her painful life story to the media.

Hi Ya.

Thanks for the letter and visit – I know you can see through my putting on a brave face.

Just because of the documentary they stopped my days out

– I'm mad. I'm mad I have these scars still on my arms.

I feel so much that I want to get it all off my chest to the Home Secretary, because I feel so strong. Julie [Emma's girlfriend in prison] and I are a wonderful couple – helping each other away from Class A substances. I want so much to go out with her Friday so we start up life together.

Harriet – they've brought her back here today as she is N.F.A. [No Fixed Abode] and she desperately needs to find accommodation. You'd love her, and when I send her a V.O. [visiting order] (not our first visit – my second) – maybe you can come along.

Please send me £40 before next Wednesday – I'm a pauper here at the moment and can't wait for private spends.

Moonie's [Emma's pet bird] as beautiful as ever – my little pal.

Still I'm going to education every day – and some days I really have to force myself. I feel it's helping me and I'm doing really well with my 'problem'. Still, I sometimes have to really shut off all the shit and pain and anger and frustration inside of me – and just try to be calm about the circumstance I'm in.

Well – believe me *I feel* I'm doing great – but some days are a bitch to get through.

Oh! Enough of me – how are you? – and Julie.

I feel like a fat, spotty body – all fat – but – that's life!

So, I'm off to put my baby to bed (Moonie). My other baby Julie got transferred back here today – to sort out an address. The first time I see her is in education at 9:15 tomorrow.

I must go – Bye for now.

Lots of Love

Moonie and Me

X   X
X   X

Saturday 27-11-93

Dear Harriet and Julie,
Hiya – How are you both? OK – I hope.

It was good seeing you again on Thursday, Julie, and I'll see you again Monday – after posting this – your visit did me good . . .

. . . and neither of you worry – I may be a bit slow – or need some reassurance from time to time – or need time to "suss the coo" – but at the end of the day – I know I am in good hands.

. . . Paul Newall – Mitch – Home Sec, Governors, Ministers, prison officers – every motherfucker who keeps me here today, and has messed with my life – "FUCK THEM".

I'm doing things *my* way now, and I've had enough . . . more than enough – but now I'm not playing their games anymore – not sitting quietly letting them keep coming and kicking me in the face anymore.

I'm going to fight for what I DESERVE . . . and I'm going to start making "people" *answer* some (A LOT) of questions –

I can't spend all night writing to you because I've about ten more letters to do – but *believe me* – the home leave incident and every little thing around it was the final kick down . . . the test of strength I needed. Right now I feel more inner strength than I've ever felt before.

Everyone keeps asking "Are you alright?" or "What have I done wrong, why you don't talk to me anymore?" . . . inmates and employees in the prison . . .

. . . I'm fine . . . But too many people have done me wrong . . . and everyone (from Howard to Ministers and Paul and Mitch and every motherfucker) who keeps me here today – and has the cheek to try to make my life more difficult for just being me and not accepting my sentence and conviction and opening my mouth – continue to do me wrong.

So, I've withdrawn completely. No more playing games –

biting my tongue and not asking questions that need to be answered – because I plan to expose the whole fucked-up, corrupt, backward – fucking cowardly – system, and what individuals and system "posses" have put me through.

Mentally – I'm preparing myself for the worst of "everything" – and physically – I'm OK.

I've been told Paul and Mitch are in the prison on Tuesday – I'll make a request to see them. But in the meantime *all I want sorted* and organised for over the next few months, and how far I'm prepared to go to get things sorted will be down on paper (and I'll send you a copy Tuesday), and also questions I want answering will be down on paper.

Enough of all that . . .

Thanks for the letter Harriet. I hope Rohit does come up soon. I need things clear in my head – and also A.S.A.P. I want the separate solicitor by my side over "the last 8 years 10 months?"

I don't want just anybody, so I'll be patient – but I'm going to be in a very vulnerable position if I have to take my "requests" to extremes – and I'm not having them mess with my life anymore.

Julie made me feel a bit/a lot letter about the filming. My life has been invaded – Trevor's and my personal business is *not* personal and private anymore – and my emotions are fucked up about having to literally open up to thousands of people over the last 11 months just to get an *appeal*.

And I don't mean just as if it's something small – I feel sick and angry – at what it's taking to make sure my appeal is listened to properly. But good must come at the end – good for me, and other people hopefully. I'm sure good will be seen in many ways at the end of the day.

Moonie is fine – he's a bloody devil though sometimes . . . poor Fran.

Holloway

Dear Harriet and Julie
What more?...

No more unescorted temporary releases and have been told I am *not* going home for Xmas.

They are punishing me for what?

They have recently sent a lifer out for the weekend (a returnee from open prison).

I AM BEING VICTIMISED.

Enclosed is a copy of Howard's letter . . . I AM NOT spending my last Xmas in jail.

Maybe I will lose your support and Rohit's – but I am sorry I can't take much more.

PLEASE COME SOON.

Love and peace,

Em X

H.M. Prison, Holloway.
Parkhurst Road,
London, N7.
November 22nd 1993

Dear Home Secretary Howard,
I don't think that I need to explain to you why I am writing to you to demand my release from prison. I'm sure you are aware of my case and the injustice of me being sat in prison.

Now I have gained the strength to fight my conviction and sentence, I will not give up until I have been listened to and tried fairly.

I am not asking for a pardon for killing someone, I am asking you to parole me until my appeal is heard.

Since I have started to work towards an appeal and speak out against the injustice of my conviction and sentence I feel like I have been victimised within the system, and now I am telling you that I have had enough.

All along I have thought it best for me to not make public

what I have been through while being in prison, because I did not want to make my life more difficult than it already is, but this time I have been pushed too far.

Not two weeks ago I was pushing along with my appeal and at the same time working through the prison system very well. I had started what I was led to believe was 'Pre-Release' from Holloway and had made all kinds of plans to do so. Along came the 'SYSTEM' . . . and knocked me down again.

I am not going to take time to tell you all the shit I have been put through since November 4th 92 . . . and even before that . . . If you have any concern or any sense of humanity you will look into it all yourself. As far as I am concerned, I am now having a separate solicitor take up what the 'SYSTEM' has put me through . . . and plan to drag 'IT' through the courts.

I'm tired of fighting my conviction, sentence and the 'SYSTEM' . . . Tired of living a life of hell.

The main point of this letter is to ask you to give me parole until I have fought and won my conviction and sentence, because I don't feel as though I can take much more within the system. I am unable to hunger strike to put pressure onto you because I would not be taken seriously due to having an eating disorder.

But I will tell you now . . . I can take very little more of this life and all the hassle. If I had the guts I would have killed myself a long time ago . . . but if need be . . . I plan to make my request again to you . . . give you a deadline date, and from then on if I am not paroled I shall stop not just solids but liquids also . . . Two-and-a-half days at the most and I shall not be aware of a thing.

If I die . . . that is my personal destiny, but at least I know there are very many people who will make sure that what I have been through will be used to avoid the same things happening to any other child/woman . . . or man.

May 18th 94
STATEMENT TO GOVERNOR KING.
FROM EMMA HUMPHREYS P32063

1) I was released from Holloway on two separate occasions for day T/R's. After the first one it was known to P.O. Davey and S.O. Wilkinson that I had taken part in a TV Documentary.

P.O. Davey told me that if D.I.P.1 had been informed by a member of staff that they wouldn't have been happy.

On my second T/R I was asked as soon as I walked out of the prison to go over my interview again. I was not happy with this, but agreed to spend the last two hours at the studio.

On return to Holloway I told Miss Wilkinson ALL that I had done on my day out, and nothing was mentioned about my contact with the press being wrong.

I applied for another T/R for 12th Nov to spend the day up in Nottingham next to my father while he was being interviewed. I was told by S.O. Dixon that further contact with Yorkshire TV was not allowed, and so she suggested I just go home for a home leave from 12th to the 14th Nov.

S.O. Dixon told me that it was arranged, my family and friends had been informed and at 3:30pm on Nov 11th I was told by her that she would drive me to the train station in the morning. I was told my train times to go to Notts and the time I should return on the 14th.

At 4:15pm the same day I was unlocked by Shuttleworth and told to go and see Dixon again. I was then told that due to lack of communication between Holloway and H.O. they had accidentally released me twice before unaccompanied. That this wasn't allowed and so I was not going on the home leave.

I could not believe what I was hearing, and so brought another inmate in to hear what was being said. This inmate is available to be questioned.

On 12th Nov I was taken accompanied to see my father to try to explain things.

I don't for one minute expect you to comprehend what I felt and am still feeling about this. My life was changed within a matter of 45 minutes. Distress was also caused to my family and friends. Let me tell you though . . . The whole matter has caused me much distress.

I demanded a meeting with the Holloway staff and D.I.P.I which was another blow. At this meeting the story conveniently changed to not Holloway or the H.O. being in any wrong but it was me that was the wrong one. The story now was that I had no right to talk with any press and so I had breached my T/R conditions, and my 'punishment' was to be no more T/R's by myself.

PRIOR TO THIS I HAD NEVER BEEN TOLD THAT CONTACT WITH TV AND PRESS WAS A BREACH OF ANY CONDITIONS OR A REPORTABLE OFFENCE AND I NEVER PRESUMED IT WAS. Why would I when at Holloway I had taken part in a phone interview with BBC Radio, and been interviewed by a journalist for the *Sunday Times*, *Observer*, *Guardian* – all taking place within the prison – and also was visited by Y.T.V. whilst they were researching? I had also taken part in an interview and filming with BBC Midlands whilst on another T/R from another prison.

I want this whole matter to be openly and honestly addressed. I deserve no punishment or victimizing.

2) On August 17th 93 I was aware that I had an appointment with my plastic surgeon. This would be a follow-up to my initial consultation a few years earlier, in regards to having self-abuse scar tissue removed from both arms, wrist to elbow.

This is a very hard subject to me. I was cutting myself from the age of 12-20, and when I stopped I was determined to have the scars dealt with so that I didn't have to see them for the rest of my life and deal with prejudice. I fought like mad with the system to be taken seriously, and was eventually taken on board by a consultant at Pinderfields Hospital, Wakefield. I was then placed on the waiting list, but was told I would wait years.

I caught wind of Holloway not wanting to take me to the appointment due to transport cost. I was fuming. But again I don't think you will be able to grasp just what grief my scars cause me.

Nowhere was I getting *any* answers, and so had to resort to screaming and shouting and refusing to move on free-flow from outside the nursing office. Luckily I did. Eventually Gov Beaston came to listen to me, called D.I.P.1 and things were in motion. The next day I was taken for my appointment.

At the consultation I was told I only had another 4-6 months wait. I was very pleased, and as time passed on I asked a friend of mine to check with the hospital if my date was coming up.

My friend called me early one morning with the devastating news that I had been given a date for the surgery and that it had been and gone. Holloway had cancelled it.

I CANNOT BELIEVE WHAT HAS HAPPENED. NO ONE EVEN TOLD ME OF THE CANCELLATION. Another kick in the teeth from the 'SYSTEM'.

So far I can find no one to claim responsibility for the cancellation, and all the receptionist at the Hospital can remember is it was a 'foreign' woman.

Last week I sent a complaint form to the Regional Medical Director, after getting nowhere within the prison.

DO I HAVE NO RIGHT TO MY MEDICAL TREATMENT? WHY ARE THESE THINGS ALLOWED TO HAPPEN?

3) Two weeks ago I and my room were literally STRIPSEARCHED. After two-and-a-half hours and finding nothing, the officers left my room totally destroyed. Almost 150 pictures all over the floor, my dried flowers crushed, my wash jug used to search through my bird sand . . . MY NICE COMFORTABLE ROOM WAS DESTROYED BY OFFICERS LAWSON SAMSON AND A NEW UNKNOWN ONE. It was a disgrace, and I have Di Shipley to witness that in her words it looked like the aftermath of an aggravated burglary. Also other officers on the level 5 were hurt for me along with the inmates.

When the officers were asked by S.O. Beddell was that what

they had done?, they said yes, and were ordered to do something about it. But it was such a mess they could do nothing but just move the mess around from one place to the next.

I was told by S.O. Bedell that I could not put any more pictures anywhere but on the pin board as it is a reportable offence. So I live in a disgustingly tatty room now. No curtain rail for window or privacy washing and toileting. Why are other cells covered in pictures?

At present I am very depressed. What they did to my room was the final straw. I am a nervous wreck and can't stand the psychological/emotional terrorism I am suffering from having all these 'upsets' happening.

I am being treated by the medical department for depression and anxiety. I have enough on my plate with working towards appeal, going through another parole review and working on my own personal problems without all these unnecessary worries.

I am asking you to step into some kind of motion to sort all this mess out.

What was done to my room cannot be undone, I will just have to try to not let it bother me so much. But I want some reassurance that officers will no longer be allowed to emotionally terrorise inmates by doing such things.

I shall be seeking compensation for every day that I live with these scars unnecessarily.

In the meantime I think it is only fair that the prison does all it can to get me a hospital appointment for removal of scar tissue A.S.A.P., even if that means the Medical Department pays for private health care for me.

I am seeking advice from my solicitor as to how to get through this very difficult time and if need be what action should be taken to guarantee that I am treated fairly and humanely by the Prison service.

N.B. In the event, Emma was unable to obtain the plastic surgery that she so desperately wanted before she died.

EMMA HUMPHREYS P32063 MAY 18/94

Dear Judges,
You will never know the full extent of abuse I have suffered,
witnessed and done to myself.

Maybe one day I will write about it all,

Maybe one day you will read about it all,

And all I want to write to you is,

Please, I beg you, don't send me back to prison.

I was ten years old when I first ran away from home.
Nothing major, but a start.

I was twelve years old in Canada when I again started to
run away, and the first few times I just got returned to my
home.

I took a drastic step one day. I used my dinner money to
buy a packet of razor blades. Sat in the school gym and cut
my wrists for the first time.

Someone took a little notice and at last I wasn't sent home.

I was twelve, running from hell,

Straight into a life of hell.

Five years later a man was dying in my arms.

Over ten years later I will stand in front of you and bleed
my heart and mind for you to just try and grasp the realities,
the effects and the damage of an abused child/woman.

It wasn't murder I did that night,

And to try to change my conviction has been a harder fight
than I ever imagined.

I ask you to look at the child of twelve in the school gym
cutting her wrists.

I ask you to look at the child of seventeen in the dock
accused of murder.

I ask you to recall Judge Jones' comments about the help I
needed.

And finally I ask you to lessen my conviction and never
send me back to prison.

It's actually twenty years late, (I was abusing myself at the
age of seven.)

But now I am receiving help, and have the most valuable team of people to help me to completely deal with the last twenty-seven years of my life and encourage me to go forward to build and have a life of my own. A life with only memories of hell.

Please release me into the care of the people I needed so many years ago.

My lover and I

She wants me to tell her
About myself and the past.

But I'm running away,
And running fast.

She doesn't understand
My moments of silence.

She has yet to find
This is not an offence.

I have things to tell her,
Moments of here and now.

I want to let her inside,
But I just don't know how.

June 1994

Some place

It's a place.
Cold, dark, steel and cement.

Anyone can go.
Criminals, the ill, lost children's children.

You need no ticket.
Just don't fit into a corner.

Dare to be you.
Someone's daughter, someone's son, just someone.

August 1994
Holloway

Emma Humphreys case: 'Landmark judgment' strengthens defence

Reception: Emma Humphreys is greeted by supporters as she emerges from the court hearing. Photograph: Tddd

DAILY Mirror
COMMENT

Opening doors of tolerance

THE freeing of Emma Humphreys is not a licence to commit murder. It is a sane and compassionate judgment.

It shows that the law now recognises that some women may be so brutalised that they are driven to kill.

That might still be a crime but it is not the cold, premeditated taking of a life which demands a mandatory life sentence in return.

Emma Humphreys has already paid a heavy price for her actions. At the age of 27, she has spent more than ten years in jail.

But her suffering did not begin on the day she was sentenced. She had by then been the victim of dreadful abuse by the man she killed.

Until very recently, the law on domestic violence was weighted towards men. Battered wives received little protection. Yet when a woman snapped, she could find herself sentenced to years in prison.

The police have made enormous strides towards dealing with violent husbands. No longer do they turn their backs on an incident, saying: "It's just a domestic".

Now the courts, too, show they are willing to accept the reality of life in these sad relationships.

Many women, through fear or financial hardship, feel they cannot walk away from them.

They need protection and sympathy. Yesterday was a historic day that showed they are now beginning to get both.

News

VIOLENCE VICTIM EMMA WINS MERCY OF JUDGES AFTER SPEND

Woman d to kill is

By NICOLA DAVENPORT

A WOMAN who served 10 years behind bars for murdering her brutal boyfriend walked free after a historic victory in the High Court yesterday.

Emma Humphreys's jail hell began when she stabbed to death the man who had beaten, raped and abused her.

It came after three judges listened to her pleas for mercy. Dazed and shaking, 27-year-old Emma led into the arms of supporters and asked: "Is it all real?"

It was her first taste of life outside prison since she was jailed at the age of 17 for the murder of Trevor Armitage, 33.

Emma killed Armitage with a single stab wound to the chest at his Nottingham home.

Judges yesterday allowed her appeal — substituting a charge of manslaughter for murder — after considering the horrifying catalogue of violence she had endured.

In the dock she clutched a pale pink rose — a gift from her woman partner. She was pale and painfully thin in a white mini dress and beige jacket.

"I don't know how I'm feeling. I'm just overwhelmed," she said afterwards.

"I just want to get away from all this and let it sink in that I am free."

She broke down in tears as a message of goodwill was brought to her from Sara Thornton, 38, who is still behind bars for killing her violent husband in 1990.

Provocation

Miss Thornton said Emma had inspired her to keep fighting.

Experts said Emma's case was a crucial legal precedent that could open the way for other appeals.

It hinged on the long-term provocation that Emma had suffered.

The judges also ruled that her history of mental instability should have been taken into account at her trial at Nottingham Crown Court.

Last night Emma enjoyed her first moments of freedom with supporters who had fought a two-and-a-half-year campaign for her release.

She will have intensive therapy to heal the wounds of the past 10 years and hopes to take up a career as a writer.

Emma, a teenage prostitute when she was convicted, was greeted outside court by her partner of two years, Julie Symmis. They met while they were in Holloway.

Julie, who was released ten months ago, said: "I'm really really happy.

"Emma needed to get out of prison today. I don't think she could have stood much more."

The appeal came after a campaign by Justice for

STABBED: Trev

FIGHT TO REFORM DC

THE Emma Humphreys case highlights the battle by civil liberties and women's groups to reform domestic murder laws.

Campaigners believe yesterday's victory is the first step towards changes in the 1957 Homicide Act, which would ensure that violence suffered by battered women is taken into account at their trial.

Under present law, a killer can only use the defence of provocation if there was a "sudden and temporary loss of control" — which rules out women who attack their partners after years of abuse.

A number of battered women serving se

Women The woman, Hel said: "The momentous one which worldwide.

"It is proof justice is su which has cre climate wher ing effects of women are su

The group women would ecstatic. But

Emma's c hellish — r marks on her permanent re

VICTORY: Emma yesterday   Picture: HARRY DEMPSTER

LIVES

MIRROR WOMAN, V

freedom is a dr

Woman who stabbed violent partner freed

...NER MILLS
Affairs Correspondent

...serving 10 years and there ...is in prison for killing her ...drunken partner, Emma ...phreys walked free from ...urt of Appeal — cleared ...der, and advancing the le ...hts of battered women.

...nervous and very emo- ...al, she appealed for the ...mes she is engulfed by dozens of ...ring women and children ...in the courts.

...campaigners will turn ...ention to the cases of 70 ...women serving jail sen- ...for killing brutal partners ...bands – including Sara

Thornton, whose case first put domestic violence on the political and law reform agenda.

Yesterday, led by the campaign group, Justice for Women, they immediately called on the House Secretary to review each case in the light of the appeal court ruling which quashed her murder conviction and substituted a verdict of manslaughter on the grounds of provocation.

Lawyers said the judgment strengthened and clarified the defence of provocation on behalf of victims of domestic violence driven to kill. It spelt out for the first time that not only must trial judges detail any history of abuse, they must also analyse and explain its significance to the jury.

Further, it underscored an earlier Court of Appeal ruling that personality traits – such as "battered women's syndrome" – and any effects on behaviour, should be taken into account when considering provocation.

...en ...ed

...

Trial judge gave 'fundamentally flawed' direction on Humphreys' 'abnormal personality'

Rohit Sanghvi, Miss Humphreys' solicitor said: "This is a landmark decision. It means that in future, if there is a doubt, judges must leave cases of abuse and battered women to the common sense of the jury."

The three appeal judges had been told Miss Humphreys, now 27, had led a tragic life of family breakdown, care and teenage prostitution. She had started drinking and taking drugs, running away from home and had slit her wrists many times.

In a letter to the judges written from prison, she said she took 12 and a half hours after she first cut her wrists. "Someone took a little notice and at last I wasn't sent back home. I was 12 and running from hell." At 16 she turned to prostitution.

A year later, in 1985, she was found guilty of stabbing to death Trevor Armitage, a drug addict twice her age who had picked her up off the streets and subjected her to months of brutality.

... rapes and verbal abuse. He had previous convictions for violence and, said the appeal judges, "a predilection for girls much younger than himself".

But despite his violence and his demeanour that she continue to work as a prostitute, he had been the only person in her life to tell her he loved her – adding to her confused life.

On the night she killed him, they had come in from a pub where he had been drinking with his son and some male friends. On the way home, he had promised them a "gang bang", causing her grave distress. She went upstairs armed with two knives and slashed her wrists.

Armitage's reaction when he found her was to undress in anticipation of having sex and must be about the "pathetic attempt" to cut her wrists. She plunged the knife into his chest, penetrating his heart.

Lord Justice Hirst said that on the night in question through was the cumulative provocation: the drunkenness, the threatened "gang bang", his relentless taunting at an unwanted threat of sex and, finally, the "wounding taunt" about her cut wrists – providing the final trigger which caused Humphreys' self-control to snap.

Lord Justice Hirst said the trial judge had failed properly to direct the jury on the cumulative effect on Humphreys of her history, and that they gave "more historical recital, devoid of analysis or guidance, and that was not sufficient".

Sitting with Mr Justice Kay and Mr Justice Casalet, he concluded that the trial judge had also given a "fundamentally flawed" direction when he told the jury to ignore evidence of Humphreys' "abnormal personality" – a trait which had developed out of her "miserable" history. This included immaturity and the attention-seeking habit of cutting her wrists. "It was clearly open to the jury to conclude that the provocation of English led to the killing brutality hit directly at this abnormality, and was calculated to strike a very raw nerve," he said.

At a press conference after the hearing, Miss Humphreys vowed to fight for further changes in the law, alongside the women who campaigned for her. In the meantime, she is to receive counselling and help to her rebuild her life.

...abused Emma ...R LAW

...lling their part- ...... for Women ...se of Kliengelt ...... after appeal ...r sentence for ...anslaughter, and ...is left.

...ving sentences ...olving violent men. ...rk Ashby and ... were backing the ...il parties for ...ghting for reform.

...of law complication, ...he who hired her ...esperately ...r 13, Emma made ...more suicidal high. ... switch ... some enormity and ...to the streets as a ...crime. ...mpart the proof ...more in used ... was a brutal bully ... I, who refused to ...hem, he raped her. ...hen again though ...and she plunged ...his chest.

Now I can start my life again

I'M FREE: Jubilant Emma yesterday

HOOKER Emma Humphreys, who stabbed her evil lover to death, was dramatically freed from jail by Appeal Court judges yesterday.

The blonde killer should NEVER have been convicted of murder for stabbing the bully-boy fiend — who beat her for money to buy drugs.

Emma gasped as she was finally released after 10 years behind bars.

She said outside court: "I now want to start a new and positive life.

"But really after 10 years in prison what's happened to me today hasn't sunk in yet. I am overwhelmed.

"I need to get in touch with my feelings. Just let me have a peaceful life from now on."

Emma plans to attend a rehabilitation centre to get support and counselling before making her way in the world.

Hundreds of women supporters outside the High Court — who had fought a bitter campaign for her freedom — clapped, cheered and sang with delight. Emma

JAILED: Red light girl Emma at 17

■■■ PETER BOND

was just 17 when she was convicted at Nottingham Crown Court of murdering pimp and lover Trevor Armitage.

She maintained from the day of her arrest that Armitage had provoked her beyond human endurance. She was regularly battered, taunted and

mentally terrorised by the 33-year-old brute.

Finally, she snapped when the drunken thug threatened to subject her to a gang bang with his pals at his home in Bulwell, Notts.

She picked up a knife and rammed it into his chest.

The blade sliced through his heart.

Emotional reception: Emma Humphreys is greeted by supporters as she emerges from the court hearing   Photograph: Tiddy Maitland Titterton

Part 3

Life After Prison

Emma on her first holiday, in Tuscany with Julie, Harriet,
Cheryl and Rosie, June 1998.

5: Not a Suicide Note

A few months after Emma's death, on the anniversary of her birthday, October 30th 1998, we organised a memorial service that was also to become the first of the annual Emma Humphreys' Memorial Prize events. Below we reproduce an account written by Harriet Wistrich, intended to 'explain' the circumstances leading to Emma's death to those attending the service.

When Emma died in July this year, a number of people asked me, "what happened?"

For those of you here who didn't know Emma – except, perhaps, through having supported her campaign for justice at the Court of Appeal three years ago, or seeing the media coverage – Emma's tragic death at such a young age may have come as a great shock to you. Sadly, for those of us who knew Emma well, whilst her death was terribly shocking – and certainly not inevitable – it was a possibility that we sometimes dreaded.

While there can be no explanation for Emma's death, I want to describe a little about the pain that she lived with, and her constant struggle to get through each day. In my mind there is no doubt that she wanted to continue living, but she may not have fully appreciated how close to the edge she lived her life.

I first met Emma in January 1993, seven years after she was imprisoned for life, and I had what turned out to be the honour of recording her life story and working directly with her in preparing for the appeal. During that time we often came into conflict with the prison system, and sometimes I wondered whether we were doing the best thing for Emma. But she was always determined that the only way she was coming out of prison was after she had cleared her name and proved that she was not a murderer.

Nonetheless, even after the great victory at the Court of Appeal, Emma continued to be racked with the guilt of having taken someone's life. However much she accepted on a rational level that she had acted under extreme provocation, she was never really able to forgive herself, and she always felt that her case was much less deserving than those of all the other women who we campaigned for.

It was that guilt, together with all of the other damage that had been done to Emma, which made living such a constant struggle. She had witnessed and experienced horrific violence at home at the hands of her stepfather. She had run away, and as a teenager had lived between children's homes and on the street, being abused as a prostitute. By the time she was 16 and living with Trevor Armitage, she was already seriously damaged.

Had Emma not had the misfortune of being represented by about the most inappropriate possible solicitor, and having to face a criminal justice system that was not attuned to issues of violence against women, perhaps she would have received help in coming to terms with the events leading to her murder conviction. Instead, she was incarcerated for life in prisons that dealt with her internal pain by sedating her with medication.

By the time of Emma's release ten years on, she was addicted to an horrific cocktail of medication. Because she came out of prison through the appeal process, the prison system took no responsibility for providing for the difficult transition to freedom. Instead Justice for Women (and Linda Regan in particular) had to set up the links with social services and seek to ensure that Emma was not suddenly without the medication that she had come to rely on. Julie, myself and Sarah Maguire provided our home for Emma in the first few weeks following her release, until a place became available at a residential therapeutic community.

During the first week of Emma's freedom, we all came to the quick realisation that the life outside prison Emma had yearned for for so long was also terrifying to her. Within five days of her release Emma was in the Whittington hospital, having overdosed on chloral hydrate. During the first year-and-a-half of her freedom, Emma ran wild. She drank and took all manner of drugs to excess; and she continued to self-harm by cutting up, through serious anorexia and by getting into dangerous situations with the sort of men who prey on vulnerable women. She was thrown out of the therapeutic community having broken every rule; she was likewise thrown out of the mental health hostel and a number of other forms of accommodation that had been found for her.

Emma constantly tested our tolerance to the limit, certain that eventually she would prove that she didn't deserve our love. She came quite close to succeeding one night, when we had to make the painful decision to turn her away from our house at 5am with nowhere for her to go.

Things began to change after she was raped by a stranger. Perhaps Emma felt that she was no longer invincible, and she started to reduce the risks that she had been taking with men. Also at this time, social services agreed to find her her own flat. This was always what Emma had wanted most, and although we were all deeply concerned about whether she would be able to look after herself, it mattered too much to Emma to have her own home after the years of institutions.

In the last fifteen months, Emma lived less than a mile away from our home. We were able to maintain very regular contact with her, and she formed a special bond with our friend, Rosie. Most Sundays, Emma would come round for the day, and we spent Christmases and birthdays together. I believe that Emma at last began to trust us, and accepted that we would remain in her life. She also started to rebuild her relationship with her father, John, and enjoyed regular visits from him and her brother Matthew.

Life, however, continued to be a struggle for Emma. She

coped by obliterating painful thoughts and memories with drink and her medication. Unfortunately, her GP provided medication on demand, and when she ran out early of her week's supply, he would give her more. We were desperate to do something about this, but Emma didn't want to change her GP because she knew that she could always get what she wanted from him.

Three weeks before Emma died, myself, Julie, Rosie and Cheryl took Emma on holiday to Italy. I shall never forget the look of ecstasy on Emma's face as she looked out of the aeroplane window over the clouds. During that week in Italy, I was fully confronted with the serious danger she was in as a result of the amount of medication she was using. For three days Emma could barely get out of bed, and her body seemed almost to ooze toxicity. But we had a lovely time together nonetheless. On our return, Cheryl and Jane arranged to take Emma to a different doctor, who told Emma that she could help her to begin to detoxify. But Emma was frightened to give up her crutch.

Rosie was the last person to see Emma alive. On Thursday 9 July, as usual, Rosie spent the day with Emma. Emma was feeling a little depressed, and Rosie lectured her about cleaning up her flat. Emma also asked Rosie to post a letter to Tom Sheerin, Emma's writing teacher at Holloway prison, asking him if he would help her to write her life story. On the Friday, none of us could get through to Emma on the phone. On the Saturday morning, Julie and I went round to Emma's flat. We took spare keys, and when we got no reply to our knocks on the door, we used the keys to get in. Emma was lying in bed, curled up on her side, as she always used to sleep. She had been dead some hours; we don't know exactly how many. But we know that she had clearly got up at some time on Friday, because she had cleaned up her flat as Rosie had advised her. There was liquid left in the bottle of chloral hydrate, therefore clearly indicating that it was another accidental overdose. Tragically, on this occasion, nobody got to Emma in time.

Looking back five years later, a question I often ask myself is, was Emma's death inevitable?

When Emma was in and out of A & E and mental health wards during the three years following her release from prison, as a result of overdosing and other acts of self-harm, I encountered on more than one occasion a kindly mental health social worker called Roger. When I asked him despairingly, was there anything that we could do to steer Emma away from this down hill destructive path she appeared intent on taking, he would shake his head and say, "it's as though she's writing a long suicide note."

Like some horror story repeating itself, the day after Emma's funeral I found myself back at the Whittington hospital, with the same social worker, Roger, and members of Emma's family. This time we were discussing Abigail, Emma's younger sister, who had come from Canada for the funeral, and who had made an attempt on her life by slitting her throat in the bed and breakfast at the top of our road. Abigail was not fit to fly back to Canada as scheduled, and she needed professional care and support. Roger asked whether there was anyone from Justice for Women who might be able to look after her? Again he described her condition as "though she is writing a long suicide note".

Emma's untimely death, however, was *not* inevitable, but can be attributed to the failure of a range of agencies who, had they intervened appropriately at the time, might have prevented the accumulation of damage to Emma's life:

As an abused child in Canada, Emma was failed by the system. The authorities were in loco parentis and had a duty to protect and care for teenage Emma, and yet she was raped and abused in prostitution and pornography. Instead of accepting responsibility, they blamed Emma herself, which she must have been experienced as a double betrayal.

Having already experienced abuse by her stepfather, it is understandable that Emma started internalising this and abusing herself. It is also unsurprising that she became anorexic, as a way of desexualising her body by attempting to return it to a childish state. Throughout Emma's life, the institutions that she came into contact with reinforced the normalisation of abuse rather than challenging it.

Emma was failed again by the system in Canada when she tried to return from the UK because she was homesick. She was a minor, Canada was the only home that she had ever really known, and the authorities had been in loco parentis to her – her father in England had never had any formal responsibility for her. Yet the Canadian authorities refused Emma re-entry and deported her, blaming her for being undesirable, which again was a double betrayal. This reinforced Emma's lack of self-esteem and her internalisation of the abuse that she was suffering.

In the circumstances, it was inevitable that, as a friendless, abused, homeless teenager, Emma would be abused again. As a teenager prostituted on the streets of Nottingham, Emma came into contact with the police on many occasions. They were also called to the home where she lived with Trevor Armitage, yet no referral was made to social services. When Emma was prosecuted for the criminal damage to Armitage's home, she was released by the court into his 'care'. Four days later, she had killed him.

Emma was then failed by the criminal justice system following her arrest for murder. Provided with a duty solicitor with whom Emma was unable to communicate, it was unsurprising that she refused to give evidence at her trial and was consequently convicted of murder. Yet it was clear to the court that she was a vulnerable young woman, the judge at trial commenting on sentencing that he hoped she would receive the help she badly needed.

If the prison system was to help her, they too failed her badly. Whilst in its care, she was introduced to hard drugs, given outdated and unsuitable prescription drugs to which she became addicted, and was sexually harassed by at least one male member of staff. Emma was also denied the right to grow and mature and was not taught any of the independent living skills that she needed. Rather than the system taking responsibility for this, Emma was punished, which again was a double betrayal and reinforced her internalisation of the abuse and her low self-esteem still further.

Following her release from prison, Emma was then poorly supported by the health and social services systems. By this time, Emma's ability to conform with any form of institutional-isation was confounded by her rebelliousness. Emma needed intensive and skilled professional support, but again the system failed to provide it.

Despite all of this, Emma was able to find her own voice and truth, to find exactly the women that she needed to help her, and to force the system to admit that they were wrong in labelling her a murderer rather than a victim. She was also, through her honesty and her determination to help stop the same thing happening to others, to improve the lives of thou-sands of women and children.

Emma displayed an extraordinary strength in being able to do this, when the vast majority of people in her situation would have lost hope long before their teenage years were up. At the point when she died there is no question that she would have killed herself. Rather, she had found a family and a home, and was beginning to make positive decisions about her future. If just one of the system failures detailed above had been reversed, it is quite possible that Emma would still be alive today.

Harriet Wistrich

Freedom

What does it mean?
It means that I can get up in the morning
And not be afraid
Llike I was as a child
Like I am in my confinement
What will hit me today?
I hope to wake up without anxiety
Wake up slowly or fast
Whatever the day feels like.

If the weather is fine
I shall sit outside
And have a cup of coffee
And a cigarette
I'll brush my teeth first
But I will take it all slowly.

Won't be sat
Like my life depends
On the shout of medication
Eight tablets for my breakfast.

I'll enjoy my coffee
May even be eating
A small something in the mornings
But I doubt it
Old habits are hard to break.

If it's not fine outside
I'll sit somewhere fresh
Or even jump back into bed
I'll be fresh
Because I'll have been
Bathing and washing
With toiletries I choose
And when I want to.

I don't think buying
A paper every morning is for me
But I would love fresh flowers
Every day
Pick them myself
Or go and buy some.

Where to Now?

Where will it lead me to
This new and exciting existence?

I have opened up locked doors
And I'm coming running out.

I feel a buzz off my adrenalin
And a calmness that flows.

This soul is carefully guided
By a leader just discovered.

Up in the heavenly skies
My eventual exit to paradise.

She watches, she protects me
And now we live as one.

As myself my whole
Have completed my tests.

For now and forever
Alive and complete.

Living in the light
Not dying in the dark.

August 1994

Emma's last Christmas, enjoying Julie's Christmas dinner, 1997.

6: Fly Like an Eagle

To love is not to give of your riches
but to reveal to others their riches
their gifts, their value,
and to trust them and their capacity to grow.

So it is important to approach people
in their brokenness and littleness
gently,
so gently,
not forcing yourself upon them,
but accepting them as they are,
with humility and respect.

(Jean Vanier)

Emma taught me a great deal about love, about honouring the person before you, whoever they are, wherever they come from. She could attract people from all walks of life: friends in high places, friends in low places. Some would say that that was a symptom of her abused childhood, that her vulnerability attracted some very dysfunctional predators. That was often true: she was frighteningly vulnerable at times, and predators crawl out of the woodwork from all walks of life.

But Emma also attracted a monstrous regiment of loving women because of who she was, not just because of the cause that she came to represent. She was generous to a fault; her capacity to love in spite of the cards she'd been dealt as a child still amazes and inspires me.

Emma lived in Wells Street, in a Hackney hostel for homeless people, for some months after her release. It was a seedy rabbit warren, filled with some of the most defeated and broken remnants of humanity. Her nearest and dearest friends were working hard as a team to get her out of there and re-housed as soon as possible. I was part of that support network for Emma, and this involved some scrapes along the way.

I treated Emma to her first hot toddy en route to an appointment at the DSS in Wilton Way. We'd arrived to find a tumultuous queue at the counter, the ticketing machine pulled off the wall, and the usual beleaguered Hackney reception staff frothing at the mouth. Only Hackney Council can produce such style in customer care. We waited and waited, only to be turned away.

Emma was instructed to go to the nearest solicitors and get a signed letter confirming who she was, as she had no National Insurance number. She was a bit fazed, so we left and went to the nearest pub. Emma was a wild card. She loved the thrill of the unconventional, and a hot toddy over the fireplace beat the hell out of hustling for a home in the middle of another Monday morning.

Two hours later we returned to try again, complete with solicitor's paw print, and reminded the staff that we had an appointment. Emma was seen briefly by Mick, who refused to meet her eye, wrote a few notes and dismissed her with some perfunctory remark. Oh, the letter was fine, yeah, but he needed a National Insurance number. The notes before him gave a clear indication that Emma had just been released from prison after ten years. I wanted to tell him why. I wanted him to know her story. But more than anything, I wanted him to show some respect and to have some compassion.

I've never been good with queues in small airless seed boxes, and I'd say I'm less good with arsey white blokes with a social skills bypass. I've been through my own trials with Hackney Council, and the whole procedure is utterly demeaning and demoralising in the extreme, feelings that I began to express in no uncertain terms.

Emma was superb. She leant forward slightly and whispered to Mick: "My friend's getting really upset. No, really upset..." She turned and took both my hands in hers and said: "Julie Mac, this is stressing you out. You wait outside, I can handle this!" She showed me to the door and dealt with the Neanderthal herself.

When Emma was finally rehoused in Crouch End, she began the slow and shaky road towards rebuilding her life. She loved having her own front door key, and shopping in the local shops, where she worshipped. She became a regular at The World's End Café, where she was always received like one of the family.

I spent hours with Emma getting the flat to feel like home. I was benefiting from the kind of hyperactivity that only medication can induce: I painted feverishly in the living room, even as Rosie and Emma were watching a movie, until Rosie would have to get up and move, and Emma would say: "Don't sit still Rosie love, Julie Mac'll have you painted!"

My mother gave her a vivid red Wilton carpet that we found somewhere in Liverpool. Emma's Dad, John, came down from Nottingham and decorated the kitchen in fresh greens and yellow. Harriet and Julie helped her to choose a beautiful bed. My friend Madinah and I donated an artists' drawing desk that had been reclaimed from a Brighton college.

Emma wanted to write again. The sap was rising, and she was getting ready to tell her story. The desk was an incentive to get her going. But I'd forgotten the chair. Emma never let me forget that. I still have her answerphone message berating me for forgetting "that fucking chair!"

Emma's warmth was like a harbour, and her home swiftly became a place to dock. There were regular house warmings, with far too much to drink. On the two occasions when I stayed over with Emma, I was amazed to discover that she had lifted me into bed. She was six stone next to my ten!

We spent our time swapping stories over drinks; we'd sit into the early hours and talk about life and death, the hardships and the dreams. Emma found it difficult to come to terms with the fact that she had taken a life. No matter how viciously cruel Trevor Armitage had been to her, how violent he had been to her, he was a living being. She was such a gentle soul, who would rather sulk than get angry. Oh, she could be high maintenance at times, but her gentleness and warmth were her strongest qualities.

Gradually her flat became a home, filled with her favourite books, CDs and videos. She had two images in her living room that were quite different from the rest: one was of dolphins swimming in the deep blue of an ocean scene; the other was of an eagle in flight. I asked about the eagle in particular. Emma had read many books on philosophy and alternative religions whilst she was in prison; she had developed her own eclectic spirituality. I wondered what the eagle meant for her? I was struck by the strength of the eagle in flight, and its isolation. Emma simply said: "We're all alone with ourselves you know, we're all doing time. But when I die, if I come back, I'd like to be an eagle!"

I have never forgotten that image, nor Emma's dreams. Her clarity and insight was breath-taking at times, and sometimes she could be hopelessly naive. But her courage to fight her own corner, to make something of her life and to stand up for women like herself, was astounding. She remains an inspiration to many women who have faced inordinate odds against them. It is what inspired me to write Emma's song: *Fly Like an Eagle*. I'll leave you with the lyrics below.

Yours was not an easy life and you never got to choose
You skated on the thinnest ice, I was so afraid you'd lose
So afraid you'd lose, I was so afraid you'd lose
You skated on the thinnest ice, I was so afraid you'd lose

Once while we were dancing,
You said: I can't be free
While the demons that I'm warring with
Are running loose in me
Yes the demons that I'm warring with

They're running loose in me
Oh the demons that I'm warring with
They just won't let me be

Everyday was an uphill road and the weather wasn't kind
You had loving friends here at your back
But too much on your mind
You had too much on your mind
Too much on your mind,
Loving friends here at your back
But too much on your mind

(Chorus)
Emma, the hurting's over, your struggle's finally done
So fly like an Eagle close up to the sun
Fly on home to freedom
There's no more need to run
Fly like an Eagle close up to the sun
Fly on home to freedom
There's no more need to run

The vultures ate you piece by piece
And the battle took its toll
They defiled you and devoured you
But they couldn't reach your soul
No they couldn't touch your soul girl
They could not touch your soul
They defiled you and devoured you
But they could not reach your soul

So you fought hard for your liberty
Though they left you just three years
You stood your ground against all odds
Filling rivers with your tears
You filled the rivers with your tears, rivers with your tears
You stood your ground against all odds
Filling rivers with your tears

(Chorus)
Emma, the hurting's over, your struggle's finally done
Fly like an Eagle close up to the sun
Fly on home to freedom
There's no more need to run
So Fly like an Eagle close up to the sun
Fly on home to freedom
There's no more need to run

Now death has taken your dreams away but your gentle
spirit's here
You learned to love and live at last
In courage without fear
Yes you learned to live and love at last
In courage without fear

(Chorus)
Emma the hurting's over, your struggle's finally done
Fly like an Eagle close up to the sun
Fly on home to freedom
There's no more need to run
So fly like an Eagle close up to the sun
Fly on home to freedom there's no more need to run
Fly like an Eagle close up to the sun
Fly on home…
Fly on home…
Fly on home to freedom
There's no more need to run

Julie McNamara

The Smell of the Blood

At seven years old I picked chunks of skin out of my hands
The smell of blood must have been there then.
Linda made me lie flat on my back one day
The smell of blood was there then.
I've been alone in places and smelt blood when it was not
around.
I've cut my arms since the age of twelve
Lots of blood there.
A man with a knife wound died in my arms at seventeen.

When I went through my breakdown
The cocoa was blood on the clothes in my sink
The smell was there
I threw the clothes away.

I've been an anorexic
I've been a bulimic
I've been a compulsive eater
Compulsive washer
I do a lot physically in my sleep
Even abuse myself.

I've been, abused and travelled on.
I don't remember burning myself the first time
It happened in my sleep or a blackout
The next time I did remember doing it.

I put four cigarettes out on my arms at the weekend.
I needed to leave myself
First the pain
Then the numbness
Then nothing.

Someone heard me scream,
But I think I'd gone by then.

Words

Thousands of words
Running around my head
I try to speak them — let them out
But they don't get out
In the usual way.
Good days, they get out
Through my fingers
And a pen.
Bad days I know well —
All the words get out
Through a cut on my arm
Or too much washing
Or too much eating
Or not eating at all
Silence is with me
We don't communicate at all.
The time we spend together,
There's a war
In my head.

November 1994

The Pit

Is it the come down,
To face reality once more?
The bottomless pit of my existence.

There are no bruises to see,
No scar tissue, no healed wounds.
You will see nothing to tell you.

About the historical remains,
Of what was once a solid mind.
Before the wars in my personal hell.

August 1994

Emma and Rosie, on holiday in Tuscany with Julie, Harriet
and Cheryl, June 1998.

7: For Emma

It was Thursday 9 July 1998, and I rang Emma as usual in the morning. She had been knocking herself out on chloral at the beginning of the week, and had felt too depressed to see me on the Tuesday and Wednesday. The chloral hydrate she took to help her sleep at night had also got a hold on her through the day, so much so that she was unable to speak. It was difficult to make any sense of what she was saying, so I told her that there was no point in my coming over to see her if she was going to be 'out of it'. When I spoke to her later on the Thursday morning, I wasn't sure what state she was going to be in. Her response was slow, but very quiet.

I asked, "What's the matter, Emma darling?" "I don't know," she replied. She sounded really down. "I'm depressed, but I don't know why." "Do you want me to come over to see you?" "No," she said. This was not like Emma, not to want to see me; she must really have been depressed. I would see her most weekdays, and every Sunday at Julie and Harriet's home, and for once she was saying she didn't want me to visit. I knew that she was very stressed out about having to make a statement to the police the following Tuesday about an ex-boyfriend who had raped her, and knew that this was why she was knocking herself out, so she didn't have to confront it. I agreed to phone her in the afternoon. I feared that she would take more chloral.

I eventually rang her back about 1pm. "How are you feeling now Babes?" "Depressed," she said. She didn't sound as slurred by this time. I was pleased she hadn't taken any more of that bloody chloral. I asked her what it was that was depressing her? "My kitchen's a mess, and there's so much washing-up." "Would you like me to wash up for you?" "Yes," she replied. She seemed to perk up a bit, and I was relieved that she wanted to see me. Usually she looked forward to seeing me every day, and I would also take Peggy, our dog, over to keep Emma's cat, Tiger, company. I praised her for not taking any more chloral, and she was sounding less depressed.

When I arrived at her flat she greeted me at the door, and we hugged and kissed in greeting. She was in the middle of talking to Tracey, her Community Psychiatric Nurse (CPN), who visited once a week. I said that I would get on with tidying the kitchen while she spoke to her. I could see why Emma's kitchen was depressing her – she'd let the washing-up pile up so much that I think I boiled the kettle for hot water about four times. I could hear Emma starting to cry, and heard her telling Tracey about Rico, the man she had accused of raping her. I thought it was better to stay in the kitchen until she had told Tracey everything. Emma eventually got up and came in to the kitchen; she smiled when she saw how spotless it was. We went back into the living room and I greeted Tracey.

Tracey spoke to Emma about starting to eat more, and advised her to cut down on the chloral. By this point Emma was beginning to feel more positive, and we talked about her eating a little more each day. When Tracey left, Emma said that she wanted to go to the shops to get some food; she said she felt better that the kitchen was tidy. I would constantly go on to her about her eating more, and a lot of the time she would only eat something if it was put in front of her. However, it was her decision to buy the food this time. She also told me that she thought the chloral was depressing her, and agreed she was taking more because of having to make a statement about Rico on Tuesday.

I asked her, was she going to be OK to do that by then? – she was determined to be all right, and promised me that she would be. Emma had cheered up so much that she seemed to get a burst of energy from somewhere. We agreed to go into

Crouch End to get some food, and she wanted to post a letter to Tom, her writing teacher in prison, asking him for guidance to start writing her life story. Unfortunately, Emma insisted on picking up another prescription for chloral from the local GP. This was a debate that Emma and I had virtually every day — she had run out again and yet she'd had two bottles of chloral already that week: already double the dose allowed for seven days within three.

There was nothing that I could do to stop her from getting yet another prescription; she was so determined because of her dependency. Even though her having three bottles of chloral in a week was technically an overdose, it was common for her to be prescribed, and take, so much on occasions. She was, after all, having a difficult week, so I agreed to take her to the surgery to get another prescription. I assumed that if she could get through the rest of the week, she would be OK to make her statement by Tuesday.

At about 2.30pm we sat and talked about her getting Tom to help her to write her life story. It was something that Emma desperately wanted to do, but couldn't seem to get started. Tom had been such an inspiration to her in prison, and Emma was a natural writer. She had written hundreds of poems in prison, but writing her life story was her priority. Emma knew that to do that would be healing to her, and an accomplishment that could help other women and children.

By this time Emma had cheered up a great deal. We sat and finished our coffee, then went into Crouch End. We strolled up the road, hand-in-hand as usual, and looked around the shops. Emma posted Tom's letter, then we went to the supermarket. She bought more food than usual, and even treated herself to fruit salad — I was so pleased that she had an appetite. I remember her having to wait a long time at the doctor's for her prescription. Her GP wasn't there, but had given permission to the nurse to prescribe Emma whatever medication she wanted.

We came out of the surgery and strolled back through Crouch End. Emma suddenly stopped and started to complain that she had a pain in her stomach. I asked her if she was all right, but she didn't reply — she just stood there looking at me. Eventually the pain subsided. Then she insisted that I was here to help her, because I was her best friend. I joked that I was her best friend but not her bloody social worker — something she knew, of course, but it did not stop her taking liberties every now and again. I took one look at her and gently hugged her.

I told her that she was a survivor of many things, and she looked at me as if she wasn't sure. Her eyes were so vulnerable-looking at times that I felt I had to reassure her in some way. To me she was a survivor; she'd been through so much in her life, and yet was still here to tell the tale. As we carried on walking, Emma forgot herself for a moment and starting flirting with her eyes — not with me, but with a woman who she saw in the street. Emma thought she was "a bit of all right", and I asked her, was she her type? "I don't know," Emma replied, slightly shy and embarrassed, and then she just giggled.

Something told me Emma was becoming more aware of her sexuality — I knew she would love to be with a woman, and I also knew I could give her everything as a friend, but not a sexual relationship. Not because I didn't love her, but because, to me, Emma was like a little girl, and only weighed just over five stone. This meant that she was too vulnerable for anyone to take advantage of her.

We started to head back home up the hill. Emma hated that bit of the walk, and eventually slowed right down: I remember grabbing hold of her and pulling her with me. I said that we were like two old ladies because we were walking so slowly. Emma thought that was funny, and eventually started walking faster. We arrived back at Emma's flat around 5pm, with both Peggy and Tiger greeting us at the door.

I made us coffee, and Emma filled the fridge. The living room was a little untidy, but she said that she would clean it up tomorrow morning, as she always felt better once her flat was tidier. She was telling me that Julie had rung her the day before, and was angry with her for taking so much chloral. I explained that we were all angry and worried, in case she might accidentally take too much and die. She totally agreed, and understood what I was saying. She said that she would take less that evening, and promised to get up in the morning and tidy up.

We went back into the living room, and each had a Bacardi Breezer. Then Emma asked me to play some music, so I put on Toni Braxton, one of her favourites. Suddenly she felt peckish, so I went into the kitchen and made her a sandwich. She ate most of it, and gave the rest to Peggy. It was after 6.30pm, so time for me to go. I promised that I would ring her the minute I got home, for a chat and to see how she was.

I left Emma reassuring her that if she got depressed again she should look forward to seeing us all on Sunday. Her eyes lit up when I said this, because she loved Sundays with her 'family'. She told me that she'd be all right and felt a bit better, and I said that I would also phone her after work on Friday. I remember thinking when I left how glad I was that I'd decided to go round to see Emma; seeing me had really made all the difference to her. Her change in attitude spoke for itself.

I arrived back at my flat about 7.30pm, and rang Emma immediately. "How are you, Babes?" I said. "I've just brought my sandwich up," she said, all sheepish. "Not on purpose?" I said, a bit annoyed. "Yes," she replied, "I couldn't help it." "That's not a good sign is it?" "No," she replied. I realised how frustrating Emma's eating disorder was – one minute the food would stay down, the next time she couldn't bear it in her stomach. I told her not to worry, and that from Friday she had to try and keep her food down, to which she agreed.

After chatting for a while, Emma said that she was going to bed. I reassured her that I would ring her as soon as I got in from work the next day. The last thing I told her was that I loved her. I wasn't to know that that was the last time I'd ever speak to Emma. As soon as I got home on Friday evening, I called her. There was no answer, so I left a brief message on her answer machine, assuming that she'd gone to bed early and saying that I'd phone on Saturday after work.

By the time that I met Emma in 1995, I'd spent the last 10 years of my life finding myself spiritually. I'd decided to get out of the rat race, and eventually gave up working as an art director for Vidal Sassoon. It was after that that I experienced two nervous breakdowns. Somehow I came through them both, but it taught me a lot about the mental health system. I had been adopted by a white family, so growing up Black mixed-race in a white town made life hard for me, as I often felt rejected by society.

I decided then only to work part-time as a hairdresser, so that it would give me the freedom to do other things in my life. I was sick of all the superficiality that went with the job. I was also beginning to realise that there were more important things in the world that I was concerned about, and something told me that I was destined to do better things. My closest friends were feminists and ran Justice for Women, and although I wasn't directly involved, I wanted to be able to contribute in some way.

I knew Emma exactly three years to the day. By the strangest coincidence, the very last day that I saw her was the same date as I first met her, the ninth of July. Emma was released from prison on the seventh of July, and Julie and Harriet took her back to their house to stay for a few weeks. It was Sunday the ninth of July 1995, and at last I was going to meet her. I'd been interested in Emma's case, and had heard so much about her.

Finally the moment had come, and Julie introduced me to Emma. I looked at her and said "Hello." Her eyes immediately lit up, I held my arms out, and we both hugged. Emma was very frail and fragile, she was also a little shaky. She looked so vulnerable that I felt an instant love for her. "Congratulations Emma, I've heard so much about you." Her eyes were blue and sparkling at me. "Sit down, sweetheart, and can I get you anything?"

Before I knew it, Emma and I had become long-lost friends. I remember that my hair was almost shaved, and Emma's hair was long. The minute that she knew I was a hairdresser, she asked me, would I cut her hair short and bleach it? I told her I would be honoured to cut her hair and give her a new image.

It wasn't until meeting Emma that I felt how very much I wanted to help her and to give her some spiritual guidance. I could see how vulnerable she was to the outside world, and how easy it was for men to take advantage of her. In fact, I automatically felt protective towards her – she seemed like a lost little girl at times. Emma needed love from people, particularly from other women. I felt like an important friend to her already, and I instinctively felt that she needed me. She was a gentle spirit, and I knew that we would eventually become special friends.

Emma's childhood and ten years in prison had left her with a lot of damage, pain and hurt – this was obvious for me to see. She had been a victim of circumstances, and had been abused by men all her life. I wanted to help her so much, to take some of that pain away. I wanted her to trust me and Julie and Harriet; she had to see that we wouldn't abuse her in any way, shape or form, and that she could trust me totally. I realised that this would take some time, but somehow I felt Emma knew deep down that she could and would come to trust us.

Emma was special in that, although she had so many scars, there was this bright-eyed, loveable person with a sense of humour, and she was able to laugh and make others laugh. I could see that there was a very stubborn side to her as well. When she wanted her drink or medication, she had to have it. I remember asking Julie once why Emma's speech was a bit slow, and she explained that she was taking this sleeping medicine called chloral hydrate.

Whatever impression I gave that first day was obviously good, and soon afterwards Emma was calling me her best friend. We decided to keep in contact by phone, and I would see her from time to time wherever she was staying. It wasn't until she got her own flat that I would start to see her almost every day; until then we were never really sure where Emma was from day to day until she contacted us. I was aware that she still had a lot of problems with men, and was vulnerable enough at times to let them hang around her, using her. She was always in an unhappy state, and when things really got her down, she would sometimes cut her wrists. When she got in a state I would frantically try to calm her down, and try to talk sense into her about not trusting men.

Emma was far too stubborn to take all of this in. I was afraid that she was going to end up really hurt. Slowly but surely, Emma would open up to me and tell me how she really felt deep down. The men that she met were all parasites, and I considered them to be abusers, because they all wanted sex from her. I think this is the reason why she kept cutting up. One man she had sex with was a social worker; another one was a young man who'd sexually abused children, something she did not know about until later; another was an old man who was very dirty, angry and possessive; and Rico, an Italian waster who eventually moved into her flat with her.

On the one hand, Emma was sick of men, but on the other hand, I think she needed their reassurance and approval that she was not a murderer and that she didn't hate men. Emma just wasn't strong enough to tell them to leave her alone. The problem was that she was alone within herself, and she felt that she needed men's company every minute of the day.

When Emma was eventually given her own flat, I found out that she had put Rico's name on the tenancy list. Julie, Harriet and I were all afraid that he would end up with the flat, and that Emma would become homeless. After talking to Emma, she agreed that it was a big mistake, and not only did she remove his name, but she also started trying to get him out of her flat. I told her that I would be able to see her more often once she got rid of Rico. Emma was starting to get really fed up with him. She didn't want sex with him anymore, and yet he was constantly demanding it.

At this stage Emma was very anorexic, and we were all afraid, aside from Rico, that she might die. I was sick of him using and abusing her. I couldn't bear to see him grabbing hold of her bottom and kissing her in front of me anymore. He was aware that I was a lesbian and Emma's best friend, and his jealousy would make him behave sexually towards her when I was there.

One day I'd had enough of his behaviour; I just flipped and went for him. Before I knew it we were fighting while Emma was watching: the whole incident became very ugly. Rico ended up punching me in the head, and I lost my balance. The next minute I was thrown on to the couch, literally on top of Emma. As he was hitting me, Emma started screaming for him to stop. Not only was he an abuser, but he was also violent. He eventually barged me out of Emma's flat and locked the door.

I was in a state of shock and panic because Rico was in there with Emma. I wasn't sure if he might attack her, so I called the police. For some reason, the police never arrived. When I got home, I rang Emma to check if she was all right. She was, but was worried about me. I told her I would never go and see her again while Rico was living there. After that day, things slowly started to change. Emma felt torn between me and Rico, and realised that she couldn't have both of us in her life. Deep down she knew that Rico was bad for her and she didn't want to lose me as a friend, so she found the strength from somewhere to tell him that he had to go.

However, Rico was so arrogant that he would shower her with presents and take her to the cinema, theatre and restaurants. He wanted Emma to feel that she could never do without him. Emma and I argued all the time every time that she brought his name up. He was still a bad influence on her, even when he moved out.

Emma would get depressed and talk about going to Kings Cross, or she would knock herself out on the chloral, or get completely drunk on vodka. But I would never give up hope that one day she would see sense. Nearly every day I would lecture her about men, her cutting up, her drinking, and her eating more. Somehow she managed to stop cutting up again, and although she talked of going down Kings Cross again, she never actually did. Also, she was slowly starting to cut down her drinking.

Six months before Emma came out of prison, Harriet had told me that she loved listening to music, so I decided to record her some tapes. I chose some special music, hoping that it would lift her and give her some inspiration. When Emma eventually came out of prison and invited me over to her new flat, I realised that we both had an affinity with music. She had four Bob Marley posters on the wall. We both started talking about chillin' out: it was something that I did every night, mainly in the comfort of my own home. It wasn't long before I knew I had a new chillin' out partner. Emma didn't know the connection I felt I had listening to Bob Marley, but I soon told her about the reason for my now growing dreadlocks, and the dreams that I had had in the past.

This empathy between us wasn't just about music, but went a lot deeper. This instinctively told me a lot about Emma, even though we were just getting to know one another. It told me that she wasn't racist in the slightest, and wanted me to be her best friend. Maybe it was fate that we met. I always believed that things happen for a reason, and I realised that Emma was an inspiration to me and I to her. I felt that I could trust her and tell her things, and knew that she would understand. I remember us having indepth conversations about the love of music and the people that were great influences on us.

I remember telling her how much I loved Michael Jackson and how my love of music began with him, because he had a great influence on my life, particularly as a child. He was my first Black friend, love, idol, and role model; his music and his persona was such an inspiration to me that I had in fact wanted to be like him. Emma told me that she wanted to see him in concert, so I arranged to take her to Wembley Stadium. I'll never forget that day: Emma only weighed four-and-a-half stone, she was very frail and weak, and she was bringing up her food, yet still she was excited about seeing Michael for the first time.

As we got to Wembley Stadium I wasn't sure how Emma was feeling, but my instincts were telling me to look after her as my main concern. I felt responsible for Emma, and I so much wanted her to enjoy the concert. She was starting to feel weak, and had to keep sitting down on the grass. I managed to get her to eat something, but before long I had to take her to the toilet as she needed to be sick.

Eventually the music started. Emma stood up and her eyes lit up. "Where is he?" she said. "Look on the big screen, he's there." At this point Emma became fixated with him. I held her hand, and soaked up the atmosphere. This was Emma's first-ever concert, so I knew that it would feel special to her. When Michael sang *You Are Not Alone*, the atmosphere changed. I looked at Emma, but she was engaging with him. Before I knew it, tears were rolling down her cheeks. I put my arm around her shoulder and whispered something in her ear, that I was so glad she felt spiritually connected. Emma bought a huge poster of him and stuck it in the middle of her room. I told her how much the song *Black or White* meant to me, because of the racism I had suffered all my life as a Black, mixed-race woman.

Emma had started to think about her true sexuality, was beginning to develop feelings for women in a way she'd not really felt before, and said openly that she wanted to be a lesbian. Emma decided that she wanted a new, short haircut, so I styled it for her. This was a really positive change for her, and she began to gain a little bit more confidence day by day; she was feeling generally happier and better from within. I think it made her feel more independent to have shorter hair, as it made her feel less of a sex object to men. Shedding her image when she came out of prison was very important to Emma, she needed to forge a new identity for herself as a free person, and I could see that this was beginning to happen.

Every two weeks Emma would receive her giro and immediately go out and buy new clothes and new make up. She loved her glitter! And her lipsticks. I could see that she knew what she liked, but this time it was for herself and not for men. Emma was finding her own individual style in lots of ways. It made me think how particular she was – she was even the same about her jewellery and her candles and incense burning.

Emma loved all of that mystical stuff such as Tarot cards, and she was taken with some of Buddha's teachings and ideas. One day we were talking about the stars – Mars and Pluto – when Emma said that she felt like Pluto. I played the Björk track, *Pluto*, down the phone for her. When she heard it she said she felt like that inside. We both started to laugh, because it was exactly how I was feeling at the time.

We both felt Björk was unique and original and we liked her style. She was definitely an inspiration, the same way in that Celine Dion was an inspiration to Emma. When she bought the album *Let's Talk About Love*, I was pleasantly surprised. When she played *My Heart Will Go On*, it touched me so much that I would cry every time I heard it; Emma found herself doing the same. We would often sit there holding each other, listening to that song. Emma thought I was worse than her for getting over-emotional.

Even though, in some ways, we had experienced very different things in life, Emma and I had a lot in common. Our favourite film was *Titanic*, at which we both cried, and we both had a thing about music. We both loved animals too, and doted on the cat and dog. Emma used to call them 'the kids', and we spoiled them both. I gave Emma Tiger for her 30th birthday when Tiger was only eight weeks old, and Emma treated her like a baby. She constantly filled her bowl up with food, and was always giving both animals treats or leftovers. Emma needed reassurance from me that I loved Tiger as much as Peggy, and I told her that of course I did. Looking after Tiger made Emma feel more maternal.

Emma wouldn't stop going on about wanting a child, and became obsessed about it. I tried to explain to her that it would be impossible for her to have a child unless she put on a lot more weight, as she was only five-and-a-half stone. She felt determined to get healthier and gain weight, her desire was so great. I also told her that she needed to sort herself out first: Emma was so badly damaged by life that I often feared she would never be able to cope on her own without the support of friends and her father.

She once had a dream that I handed her a child, which I thought symbolised Tiger. Emma was desperate for love and the feeling of belonging herself, I know she wanted to give that back in return. Afterwards, when she thought about it, believing that she could never get to seven stone, she realised that Tiger was enough for her to deal with, and that the responsibility of a child was far greater. She realised that it was too much to cope with, and, eventually, that yearning for a child fizzled out.

Emma was slowly but surely beginning to look at the positive things that she had in her life. She had her own flat, a pet, a best friend and other special friends. She belonged somewhere at last. Emma would spend her birthdays, Christmas and summer holidays with us – she knew she had a family. She was also beginning to trust in her father, John, and her younger brother, Matthew. They lived in Nottingham, but spoke regularly on the phone, and John would visit every few weeks. John was a very caring father, who was concerned about Emma's welfare and general health. She was forming a bond with two families, and this gave her more security.

Emma desperately wanted me to meet John and Mathew. Emma had a problem in trusting men, and worried that even her father may have abused her, as everything was such a blur at times. She told me that she'd even asked him if he'd ever abused her when she was little. John was mortified, he felt very protective of Emma, and in some ways still saw her as an innocent child, who needed to be told at the age of 30 that if she didn't tidy her flat, then he wouldn't come up to see her.

When I met John and Matthew, I liked them straight away. Matthew was thirteen, but quite young for his age. He would laugh at Emma's little habits, and she also had a great sense of humour that would have him in fits of giggles. Emma didn't really have any airs and graces, and was very down-to-earth. She did not appreciate superficiality in anyone, and needed to be accepted for herself.

Emma would do all kinds of little things to test me as a friend. She would push me so far, just to see what my response was. She was clever like that. Emma needed to know that I was a real genuine person too. She was very kind-hearted, and would often give me little gifts to show how much my friendship meant to her. Our bond was becoming stronger, and she was slowly beginning to be herself with me. If she wanted to act naughty she could, if she wanted to be like a little girl then she could.

Emma especially loved Christmas with me, Julie and Harriet. She would bring her little tree and decorations with her. I remember us being like kids on Christmas morning, really excited to have so many presents to open. Emma's eyes would light up every time that she was given a present. It was like watching a child. It was the same for her 30th birthday. Her friends organised a big party for her, and invited lots of people. We bought her a mobile phone to keep her connected with the outside world when she was alone, and Tiger to be with her to stop the loneliness. It was a brilliant party for Emma, mainly because she could see how popular she was and how many people liked and supported her. We all wanted her to be happy, and to feel loved.

Once Emma began to look at all the positive things she had in her life, it gave her more security. She realised for the first time that she had a future. We began to talk about the future a lot; what we discussed gave Emma something to live for. We talked about us both writing our life stories and getting them published. I remember asking her how she would feel if she became really famous? She just laughed and quite liked the idea. "What if they made a film of your life?" I asked. She thought for a while and said: "I'd like Jodie Foster to play me, and Bob Hoskins to play Trevor." "And what are you going to call the book?" "Me, myself and I," she replied. "That's a bit self-obsessed isn't it?" I said, and she grinned.

Emma was also preparing to sue her solicitor, as she felt that he was partly responsible for her spending ten years in prison and being branded a murderer. We talked about the possibility of her getting compensation. "What will you do with the money?" Emma would have loved a bigger and nicer flat some-where, and a holiday abroad. "I will take you all on a cruise," she said with excitement. I realised that Emma was not that bothered about being rich, she just wanted to feel happy and content. She would have given her last penny away!

There were so many things that Emma wanted to achieve. She talked to me about coming off all her medication one day: "If it takes me ten years, I want to come off it completely," she said. "And I don't have any inclination to cut up anymore." I encouraged her in this. She even wanted to go into therapy to help her with the other deep-rooted problems. "One day I'd like to do some kind of voluntary work, and also help vulnerable children, and I want to help to campaign against prostitution."

I was so proud of Emma; she'd already come a long way in such a short time. It made me realise that I would never give up hope for her. We even laughed at the idea of being good friends when we were eighty, and wondered what we'd both be like at that age. We talked about religion, and agreed that God was within ourselves. We spoke of the state of the world, and about feminism. We agreed that if every woman in the world were a feminist, it would be a better place. We talked about finding our true paths in life.

I told Emma that we both had the best friends in the world, and she agreed. I think she was also becoming interested in being celibate. It suddenly dawned on me that Emma could see a light at the end of the tunnel.

When Julie came to tell me that Emma was dead, I was at work. I kept repeating "What do you mean?", then I started laughing. I was in a state of shock. I went to Julie and Harriet's, and when I realised that it was true, I couldn't stop crying. I didn't want to be left on my own until after her funeral. I had suffered a great loss, and there would be a gap in my life. One day Emma was there, the next day she was dead – how could this be? I never, ever thought that she would die. I believed she would survive, and be around for years, but it wasn't meant to be.

I began to think that there was a reason why she was taken to the other side, and that she must have been needed in the spirit world. She was only 30, and they say that only the good die young. Her death has had a profound effect on me. I had lost not only a friend, but also a soul mate. Never again would I meet someone as unique as Emma was. Meeting her and knowing her for those three years has enriched my life; I have gained something rather than lost it. I realise how important her life was, and how her death will make a change in so many ways. She was an inspiration to me, and I am a better person for knowing her. Her funeral was beautiful, I chose three pieces of music: Michael Jackson: *Gone Too Soon*, Deserée: *You Gotta Be*, and Celine Dion: *My Heart Will Go On*, our favourite.

I'll never forget the week before Emma died. I took her for an Indian meal. That night she looked me in the eyes and said that she was in love with me. I reacted with: "You're not in love with me, but you love me." Her eyes began to fill up. "No I *am* in love with you," she said softly. My eyes couldn't look away from hers, and they filled too, for I believed her. She'd finally found her identity as a lesbian, and I wanted her to know that it was all right for her to feel in love with a woman, I was truly grateful.

Emma will always be a special person – that's why her spirit lives on, and why I will always be so glad I met her.

Rosie Fitzharris

> I believe, when someone passes away, either a star is born, energy so pure, that it creates new worlds. Or as the soul releases, shatters into pieces, becoming free flowing thoughts from my mental thesis. Maybe we just don't understand spirits that still walk the land. Well, whatever the case, I believe that we all still remain to share the same space.

Lisa "Left Eye" Lopez, Supernova, 2001

Dreams

Not the ones that plague your mind in the night,
I wanna tell you about the ones that keep me alive.
Lived and living a nightmare, but not in the still of night,
I was conscious, I am conscious, it's all real,
But I dream.
I dream of laughter from within and around me,
Running naked in the rain, taking a shower from the heavens.
No one knows what it is about me,
That wakes me from the nightmares, to carry on some more,
It's my dreams.
Flat out on a hot beach, free of clothes, free of my past.
A safe place I can call home, my space, my loves.
It would make you stop and stare as you passed it.
As it'd be full of the beauty I need inside and around me.
I will always dream.

Opening Doors

I'm going in two directions
As I travel forwards.

Understanding a haunted past
While living a guided now.

Backwards or forwards
Hundreds of doors around me.

And for only me to choose
Which ones I dare to open.

May they be charcoal black
May they be plated in gold.

Only I possess the keys
To the doors in my mind.

August 1994

Afterword

Since Emma died, in July 1998, her case has been success-fully cited in several trials and appeals of battered women who kill. 'R v Humphreys' has come to symbolise crucial changes in the law in cases where the defendant has experienced sustained abuse resulting in cumulative provocation. Justice for Women continues its work on behalf of women penalised by the criminal justice system for protecting themselves against violent and abusive men. Emma's case is seen as an important landmark and inspiration for this work.

Shortly after Emma's death, a prize was set up in her name. The Emma Humphreys Memorial Prize is an annual commem-orative prize awarded to a woman or group who, through their writing or campaigning, have raised awareness of violence against women and children. It was first awarded in October 1998 to Fiona Broadfoot, who had escaped prostitution and set up an organisation to support women wishing to do the same. Since then the prize has been awarded to a number of innovative groups and individuals, and in 2002 was given char-itable status.

In September 2000 the inquest into Emma's death was heard. The jury at St Pancras coroners' court in London returned a verdict of 'death by misadventure'. They heard evidence that Emma died due to an overdose of chloral hydrate. A post-mortem examination found 23 times the recommended dose of the drug in her system.

Chloral hydrate is an outmoded medication that should not be used for periods of longer than six weeks at a maximum dose of 2g daily. Emma had first been prescribed chloral in prison, and had become addicted during 13 years of use. A report by a professor of pharmacology, read at the inquest, described the bulk prescriptions that Emma had been supplied with as being 'reckless'. In the week before her death she had requested, and been prescribed, 560ml of chloral hydrate – her normal weekly bottle would contain 200ml.

The court also heard that Emma was prescribed other medications, including the sedative Temazepan, and Modecate – a powerful anti-psychotic drug with serious neurological side-effects intended for particularly disturbed schizophrenics. She was not, and had never been, diagnosed as a schizophrenic. Emma had last been injected with Modecate a few days before she died. Chloral hydrate and Modecate are particularly inappropriate because they engender feelings of complete dissociation from the body, including loss of appetite. Emma had a history of anorexia and self-abuse stretching back to childhood, and her low body weight was a factor in her death. Emma's struggle for health was sabotaged from the beginning by the medication that she believed was helping her.

A complaint against Emma's G.P. was sent to the General Medical Council, but not upheld.

Shortly before Emma's death, in January 1998, proceedings were issued against her original trial solicitor for negligence. The claim set out how she was badly advised and as a result remained convicted of murder, thereby spending far longer in prison than she should have done. Emma was seeking damages for distress, loss of liberty, expenses and loss of earnings. Had the case proceeded, it may well have set a further precedent in law as to the basic standard of care that should be expected from criminal solicitors advising vulnerable (female) defendants. It would have been the first time that such an action had been brought by a battered woman convicted of killing her abuser. Unfortunately, the case had to be discontinued when Emma died.

Justice for Women are currently working on several cases, both pre- and post-trial, of women who killed their abusers. Emma continues to be an inspiration for this work, and remains one of the cases, and the person, that touched our lives and hearts so profoundly. This book is a thank you to Emma for being such a formidable feminist, and special human being.

Web site addresses:

Emma Humphreys Memorial Prize
http://www.emmahumphreys.org

Justice for Women
http://www.jfw.org.uk/

Peace

In a world so mistaken,
I am sure you will find what I have found
In a midnight star.
Peace.

May 1994
Holloway.